JOURNEYS

Also by Neil Cole

Raising Leaders for the Harvest (with Bob Logan)

Cultivating a Life for God

Greenhouse Workbook, Stories One and Two (with Paul Kaak)

TruthQuest

Organic Church

Beyond Church Planting (with Bob Logan)

Organic Leadership

Ordinary Hero

Church 3.0

Journeys to Significance

Church Transfusion (with Phil Helfer)

Primal Fire

One Thing

Rising Tides

PRAY

VIRAL

JOURNEYS

Discovering God's Paths of
Spiritual Formation
Building to a Strong Finish

NEIL COLE

Starling
Initiatives

PUBLICATIONS

Cover and interior design by David Provolo.

Edited by Val Gresham.

ISBN (SOFT COVER): 979-8-218-37707-6
ISBN (E-BOOK): 979-8-88940-745-4
ISBN (AUDIO): 979-8-88940-742-3

PUBLICATIONS

ACKNOWLEDGMENTS

During the summer months of 1994, I read two life-changing books. And while I was reading them, I was also reading the entire book of Acts every week. The concepts discovered in all this reading proved to be volatile ingredients when mixed.

The first book was *Missionary Methods: Saint Paul's or Ours*, written by the late Anglican missionary Roland Allen and first published in 1912.[1] I am in his debt, and I tread with much humility and caution as I set out to add anything to a subject so well treated by a scholar of his caliber.

The second book was *The Making of a Leader*, by J. Robert Clinton.[2] Dr. Clinton has devoted his life and career to discovering the paths and processes of leadership formation, and his discoveries form much of the framework of this book. Though I regret that I have never met Dr. Clinton or taken any of his classes, he has been my mentor through his writing, especially through this book. I am indebted to him for the years of hard work he invested in studying the lives of more than a thousand influential Christians to determine how a leader finishes well.

It was during this summer that I discovered the framework undergirding this book. But I couldn't write the book then. I needed to walk some of the well-worn paths that were laid before me so that I could have the ability and experience to write the book. As a result, the first version of this book was sixteen years in the making. Nevertheless, the very moment I held the original book in my hands for the first time, I heard God say He was about to take me on a whole different journey. There were even additional lessons to be learned so that I could rewrite the book as it is now. It has been an additional thirteen years since the original book came out. The one you now hold has thirty years of experience invested in its development. Thirty years of sweat and tears are found on these pages.

I owe a debt of thanks to Bob Logan, who helped me to first publish and refine these thoughts. As Barnabas did for Paul, Bob took me off the bench and put me in the game.

Thanks to Sheryl Fullerton for initially publishing these ideas in book form, even if not as fully refined and expressed as they are in this rewritten work.

For almost 20 years, Val Gresham has walked with me as a trusted editor for many of my books. I have always valued her strong input, no matter how much she advises changing and pruning my words to communicate more precisely. She done made me smarterer than I was.

Brad and Cari Fieldhouse have continued to provide a writing sanctuary, and much of this book was finished under the blessing of their loving hospitality.

CONTENTS

BECOMING A LIFELONG LEARNER
Finding Our Way on the Journeys of Life

> *In times of drastic change, it is the learners who inherit the future. The learned find themselves well equipped to live in a world that no longer exists.*
> —Eric Hoffer

> *Be imitators of me, just as I also am of Christ.*
> —The apostle Paul (1 Corinthians 11:1)

After finishing some meetings in Indiana, I rushed to the Fort Wayne airport only to find that my flight had been canceled. I was supposed to conduct a seminar on leadership formation in Chicago, but the airline had canceled the forty-minute shuttle because of adverse weather conditions.

The night sky was beautifully clear, and it wasn't even cold. Chicago was less than two hundred miles from me, so how could there be that sort of extreme weather only a short jump away from such a calm sky?

I suspected that airline officials were lying about why they had canceled the flight. My nastier self was convinced that they just didn't have enough passengers to warrant the expense of the flight and had used the weather as an excuse to cancel it. I can be such a cynic. I felt I had no other option but to rent a car and launch into the four-hour drive. It was already close to eight o'clock in the evening, and my seminar started at nine the next morning.

The drive on the toll road from Fort Wayne to Chicago was easy and uneventful, confirming my suspicions all the way. Around midnight, as I was approaching the Chicago city limits, I was talking on the phone with my wife when it started to snow. I told her the snow was pretty but certainly not heavy enough for flights to be canceled. As I entered the city, the snow was really filling the air, and the wind off Lake Michigan was gusting so hard that the snow was blowing horizontally rather than falling vertically. And the temperature had dropped considerably. It was so frigid that the snow whirling in off the lake was sticking to the metal road signs, covering up all the street names. I couldn't tell where I was or where I was going. I had to admit I was wrong with my earlier anger and cynicism.

I was effectively blind. Imagine trying to find a specific address in a large, unfamiliar city without the aid of highway or street signs. This was before GPS became a feature of rental cars or smart phones, so my clearly written down directions to the hotel might as well have been Grandma's recipe for snickerdoodles. I was alone, seemingly the only traveler lost on this four-lane highway in a snow-covered world. I felt as if I were trapped in an episode of *The Twilight Zone*—but without the signpost up ahead to tell me so. The only other person I came across was the lonely and cold tollbooth attendant, who either could not or would not help me out. Apparently, all he could do was grunt.

I pulled off the road and into a parking lot, just to think and pray—and scream as I hit the roof of the rental car in frustration. It was now after one o'clock in the morning, and I was not feeling good about calling anyone in town that late. Besides, how could I even tell them where I was?

I might not have had a human guide, but I did have access to God, who always knows the right path. After some lengthy complaints, I asked Him to help me figure out this situation.

An idea popped into my mind. I drove to a twenty-four-hour convenience store and requested a map. What good was a map, you may wonder, if I still couldn't read the highway signs? But the first step in finding your way is to recognize where you are. It is significantly helpful to find out how lost you really are. So first I had the clerk show me on the map exactly where I was.

Next, I located where on the map I was supposed to be. It is important to know what your destination is. Where do you really want to go?

Then I looked carefully at the map and meticulously counted the number of highway off-ramps and the number of streets before each of the turns I would have to make to get to my destination. I took note of significant landmarks that would confirm that I was heading in the right direction. It was a desperate but feasible plan that I was determined to make work unless and until God provided another important piece of the solution. What are the milestones and markers to discover on the path to where you want to be from where you are?

As I walked out to my car with this plan, I noticed that a limo driver was finishing pumping gas into his car. As ingenious and creative as my own plan was, God gave me a better one. I asked this veteran of the streets of Chicago if he would be willing to guide me to my hotel, figuring that since he knew the path, he didn't need the street signs. He agreed. I drove in the dark, without signs, following someone who had been down the path before—all along checking my progress with the landmarks I had memorized from the map. Let the experience and expertise of someone who has gone before you help you to find your destination.

I had spent four and a half hours driving through rural Indiana, and then another two hours to find my destination in Chicago. Never had a Holiday Inn looked so inviting.

Road signs are something we see every day, and yet we all take them for granted—until we don't have any. Life doesn't usually come with lit-up street signs telling you when and where to turn next and what landmark is ahead. That's why you need a good map of the landmarks you can expect—and, hopefully, an experienced guide.

Think of this book as a kind of map, with landmarks you can look for. Think of the apostle Paul as a seasoned veteran who has followed the path before you and can now show you the way to your final destination. Like Paul, we are called to find our own place in the unfolding journeys of our lives and to decide that nothing less than finishing well will do. In this book, I hope to point out some of the more obvious landmarks and paths of leadership formation that can guide you toward a strong finish to your life.

I do not in any way want to imply that I have lived out all the journeys that are described in this book. I hope not—I am too young to die.

But the only people qualified to write with that kind of authority about finishing well have already left this planet, leaving the rest of us to offer some ideas. Like Paul, I can say that I am still pressing on toward the goal, and like Paul, I do know what the goal is—to finish well and become more like Christ with each step of the journey. I am not Paul, but I have lived enough, watched enough, and read enough that I can put down these thoughts even if some of the final chapters are still only a pursuit for my own life.

These principles come delivered in the true story of one of the most influential characters in history: the apostle Paul. I believe the book of Acts will come alive to you, and all the epistles of the New Testament will fit into place. You will find answers to questions you may not have even dared ask as you read this narrative.

This book offers strategic missional lessons that can help you be more impactful in life, but even more, it focuses on the spiritual formation that Paul went through. He is not just an example to missionaries, theologians, and church leaders. He is an example, above all else, of a follower of Christ who demonstrates for us the paths we all must take to finish well. We can all follow him as he follows Christ.

For every Christ-follower there will be seasons when clear direction is sadly lacking and normal ways of operating are no longer useful. Lost in temporary blindness, what will you do? Giving up, making excuses, shifting blame, shouting expletives, continuing to press the accelerator in false hope while heading in the wrong direction—all these paths are ill advised. Every mile you go in the wrong direction adds two useless miles to your journey. We need to be able to depend on God for creative solutions that get us to our longed-for destination. This book is to help with just that.

If you are in a holding pattern and seem unable to make any of the progress you once hoped for, here are some important steps I learned in a freak snowstorm that can apply to your own journey in spiritual formation:

1. Pause and take a breath. If possible, find some reason to laugh, even a little.
2. Get your bearings. Where are you right now?
3. Take an inventory of your progress (or lack thereof).

4. Determine how God wants you to finish and ask God to lead you forward from where you are now, step by step.
5. Courageously follow His lead, no matter what it costs you.
6. Seek help from an experienced mentor who has gone down these paths before.

Paul is one who has walked the path and found a way home. Unlike the nearly 70 percent of Biblical heroes, he finished strong.

I believe that to understand Paul, we must first understand and love his Messiah, Jesus. Do not think that this book is about how we can become more like Paul. I am convinced that such a book would be a bitter disappointment to the apostle. No, this is a book about how to learn to be more like Jesus. As Paul became more conformed to the image of Christ with each step of his multiple journeys, so can we.

Paul the Learner

I have made it a personal pursuit to understand the explosive expansion of Christ-followers described in the book of Acts. In studying through Acts well over a hundred times in thirty years, I have discovered some aspects of Paul's developing maturity and effectiveness that I have not found reported in other books that cover his life. Most address Paul as a teacher of others, which of course he was. But I have come to see that the reason he was such a good teacher is that he was first a good learner. In showing the lessons that Paul himself had to learn to become more and more like Jesus and consequently make a bigger impact on others, I seek to show how we can all become better learners. This book should not be placed on the shelf of leadership, but on the shelf of *learnership*. This is a book about spiritual formation over a learner's entire life. It is therefore relevant to anyone who desires to be a better disciple, learn more, and increase the impact of his or her life.

The most common Greek word for a follower of Christ is *mathetes*, translated as "disciple," which means a learner. To be a disciple is to be a learner. At the core of our being, when all lesser things are stripped away from our identity, we are learners. To stop learning is to choose to no longer be a disciple of Jesus. I wouldn't wish that on anyone. We must be learners for life, for there is more than enough to learn in any lifetime.

Most books on Paul's methods tend to summarize a single strategy based on a comprehensive look at all he did. In contrast, I believe that Paul adapted and grew more effective with each journey. In some cases, Paul abandoned some strategies as he matured and embraced others that were more effective. To take all that he did and boil it down to a single method is an insult to Paul the learner.

I fear that many of us have viewed the historical passages of Scripture concerning characters like Paul through lenses that do not allow our heroes to make mistakes. We view their practices with an almost superstitious regard that sees them as infallible. I do not believe that the apostle himself would want this sort of blind devotion. In fact, it is not fair to him. When we revere him in this way, we steal his humanity from him, and he loses one of his most important qualities—his ability to adapt, learn, and mature. And if we forfeit those aspects of Paul, he ceases to be such an outstanding example for us to follow.

Paul himself seems to want to be seen as human, approachable, and not in any way superior. One word used dominantly by Paul to describe himself in the New Testament is the word *astheneia*, translated as "weakness." He uses the term 44 times in his letters, more than all other New Testament writers combined. A mentor and teacher for me, Dr. David Alan Black, called Paul, "the apostle of weakness."[1]

When it comes to examining the lives of noteworthy individuals in the Bible, we have two choices: we can view these characters as exceptional, one-of-a-kind people, or we can see them as ordinary people with an exceptional Savior. People who wish to excuse their own lack of influence often prefer the former viewpoint, but I always choose the latter. I truly believe that the stories found between the table of contents and the concordance of the Bible are there to inspire us to live better lives. If the people in those stories are too far removed from our ordinary lives, we will never even try to follow their examples. So, I have sought to understand the humanity and frailty of Paul and even highlight the mistakes he made along his journeys. I tried hard to avoid presenting him as a superhero of unattainable skills and character.

We can all learn the same lessons that Paul did and grow in our positive influence on those around us. In the end, none of us will be exactly like Paul, nor should we aspire to be. Hopefully, we will be the people Jesus desires us to be. Paul was just that, the person Jesus wanted him to be. We can all pursue that end even if we are diverse and unique because of it. What we will find is that the elements that went into Paul's spiritual formation were not at all exceptional, although the speed of his maturation and the intensity of his lessons were indeed phenomenal and, as a result, his influence is remarkable. In reflection, however, it is not so much Paul's personality, drive, or knowledge that made him exceptional—it was his willingness to follow Jesus no matter the cost and to learn with every step of each journey. That is something each of us can also do.

The Journeys of Life

It is common for people to view life as a journey, and in many ways it is. I am coming to see, however, that life is not just a single journey but several, each full of new territory, exciting adventures, and life lessons to be learned. In this book, I break down how life's journeys build toward greater meaning and significance as we choose to continue to seek the constant formation of Christ in our life.

Pressing forward means not remaining stuck in a single journey that continues to loop through the same curriculum, unlearned each time. People stuck in such a pattern will have to experience the same lessons over and over with increasing ferocity until they finally master what God intended. The names and faces in those circumstances may change, but the lesson will not change except to get more intense with each go-around. We simply cannot advance in our development without learning what God is teaching us about us.

From his study of more than a thousand Christian leaders over the course of his career, Dr. J. Robert Clinton has identified six potential phases of growth that God takes a person through to develop maturity, leadership, and a Christlike character over the course of a lifetime. In this book, I have applied that formation process to the apostle Paul. The following timeline shows Clinton's stages lined up with Paul's journeys.[2]

Leadership Formation Timeline

Phases	Phase I	Phase II	Phase III	Phase IV	Phase V	Phase VI
Clinton Stages:	Sovereign Foundations	Inner-life Growth	Ministry Maturing	Life Maturing	Convergence	Afterglow
Paul's Journeys:	Birth & Early Life	Conversion & New Life	First Journey	Second Journey	Third Journey	Fourth Journey & Beyond
NT Passages:	Philippians 3.5-6	Acts 7-13.3	Acts 13-15	Acts 16-18.22	Acts 18.23-20	Acts 21-28
		Galatians 1.11-24	Galatians 2.1-10			1, 2 Timothy & Titus

Of course, life does not follow neatly prescribed stages, with special graduation ceremonies at the end of each one to mark our passage forward and send us on our way. These phases of development are generalized and can even cross over into one another. There are also boundaries between phases, including periods when life feels stagnant. These developmental stages are best viewed in hindsight, but they must be lived in blind forward progression. And not all the stages are guaranteed for all of us.

When I teach these concepts, people commonly try to find where they are in life's progressive journeys. Many tend to overestimate their progress to date, assuming they are further along than they are. I usually say, "When you think you have found your place, move at least one phase back and start there." If this sounds harsh, I like to remind people of a few things. First, you do not become more spiritual as you progress, but simply more mature—and there is a difference. Second, the journeys spelled out in this book are by no means a guarantee for everyone—in fact, few people will ever experience the fourth journey mentioned in this book. Even the third journey is rare for people. Finally, it may be to your advantage that you are not as far along on these journeys as you are inclined at first to believe. I usually smile and say, "That may just mean that you have longer to live. Don't be too anxious to rush to the end."

This Book's Approach

Each chapter begins with the narrative of Paul's life story, unfolding the phases of development in his spiritual formation. The second part of each chapter uses the lessons he learned during that phase to explore how all of us can go through similar developmental processes. We will discover how God molds a follower at each stage of formation. Many of these ideas are not strict formulas, bound by rules or deadlines, but general observations. I may unpack a spiritual formation process that God uses (such as "isolation") in an earlier phase, but that doesn't mean it can't occur in a later phase of development. Where there are connections with Paul's own development, I do my best to point them out.

You may find that some of the descriptions are true in your experience and some are not, and that's normal. Each of us is unique and has our own journey to follow. You will likely find a great deal of insights that are indeed relevant to you. In fact, the spiritual formation processes described in this book that do not seem relevant to you will probably be few—or they may be a coming attraction in one of your future journeys.

I will conclude each chapter with a set of reflection questions to help you evaluate your own experience based on the spiritual formation process discussed in the chapter. This is not just a biography and analysis of Paul, nor a commentary on Acts, though it includes both of those elements. It is a road map for your own spiritual development and formation. Personal reflection in light of the content is important.

I try to strike a delicate balance, examining not only Paul's life and character development but also his strategy and methodology, all the while relating his lessons to the universal ones we all must learn. My intention is not to force my paradigm for mission and spiritual formation on Acts but rather to draw out the parallels from Acts and from the epistles that help illustrate these common patterns. Although I do not believe that Luke's strict intention in writing Acts was to teach these principles, we can still discover in the story many common characteristics of the maturation process. I have tried to keep this balance throughout the book, and I hope I have succeeded, but it is entirely possible that my observations are less than accurate, or that they are offered in a voice that is too certain. I am capable of mistakes. This is a resource for learning, and all good learning requires risk.

There are some unavoidable gaps in Acts that I tried to fill in a way that makes sense, based on my study of many excellent resources devoted to answering questions about Paul's life. But in the end, I had to make my own choices about chronology, geography, and the most challenging one of all, motivation. If I felt that some explanation was warranted, I included my reasoning in the notes. Whenever I have moved from clearly recorded history into speculation, I tried my best to speak in a voice that will allow for other options and opinions. This book is not a composite history but a study of the spiritual formation of a foundational character of history.

Although I wrote in a narrative style, I intend this book to be a strategic resource for both personal spiritual growth and missional strategies. In unfolding the story, I don't cite all the scriptural references for the narration, since that would interrupt the flow. You can simply follow along in Acts if you want specific "addresses" for the various parts of the story. Nevertheless, I have included references for insights gleaned from other passages in Acts and the epistles that shed light on where we are in the account. I worked hard to balance both strategy and narrative so that the book flows and is useful.

While it isn't until later that Saul of Tarsus chooses to be called Paul (the Greek version of his name), he has become known to us all by that name. So, for the sake of smooth reading, we will use the name Paul throughout the book unless it is pertaining specifically to the actions of the notorious Saul of Tarsus, such as his stoning of Stephen or his persecution of the church.

If we are to return to a life-transforming Jesus movement, we simply must take a fresh look at the book of Acts as well as Paul and his letters. We must evaluate our own experience in their light. We may also find that approaching the New Testament with a fresh perspective shines new light on its truth. We must not force our own bias or culture on the New Testament but remove lenses that were once forced upon us, lenses that have caused us to place the Scriptures into an old and culturally biased container that is no longer suitable.

We will discover some profoundly strategic lessons that Paul learned and adopted so that he could be more productive and influential with different groups, finish strong, and become more like Jesus. I have not taken anything away from the great apostle, but at the same time I have tried to demonstrate how normal his pattern of development is and how we all must journey along similar paths. I think he would prefer that treatment.

Few of us can claim yet to have the type of success that Paul has had. But all of us can aspire to go further on the journeys that deepen our faith and impact on the world around us. Not everyone is an apostle; we all have different callings to pursue—but we are all intended to grow and mature in Christlikeness and thus to have greater influence on those around us. In this very important way, we can all learn from the life of Paul. Perhaps in the days ahead, new Pauls and Paulines will arise and change our world forever.

Finishing well is not something that you do just at the end of your life—it is what you resolve to do every day you live. It takes passion and perseverance. Determine now that you will finish well or die trying.

CHAPTER 1

BORN TO A DESTINY

Discovering Early Paths That Lead to a Lifelong Purpose

God is not like a chess player casually moving us pawns around on a board. Nor is it clear until years later, if ever, what God was accomplishing in the difficulties we suffered.
—Tim Keller

God had set me apart even from my mother's womb.
—The apostle Paul (Galatians 1:15)

From a human point of view, there is nothing remarkable about Paul's birth and early life. His parents did not have angelic visitations. New stars did not appear overhead to guide people to his crib. There were no shepherds hearing angelic choirs or Magi bearing gifts from the East to his humble home. There was no indication that this man would forever leave his mark on history.

But the hand of God left fingerprints all over Paul's early life. He was born prepared for a destiny. Later in life, he understood this and commented that God had set him apart even from the time of his conception. He would find that the Lord had been preparing him all his life for his calling and for the journeys that were planned for him.

Paul's Story: Birth and Early Life

Paul was born into a devout Jewish family and grew up in the Roman city of Tarsus, in what is now Turkey, during the *Pax Romana* (the peace of Rome). Those days were not particularly peaceful for people, but the

Roman Empire had sufficiently beaten down all competitors for power and stood alone as the ruling government of the world. The Empire expanded its influence by building up its cities and increasing its roadways and shipping. As a result, the known world became smaller in many ways during that time.

Paul was born in a time ripe for the work he would be chosen to do—spreading the name and message of Jesus across the known world. The Roman system of roads provided paths for him and his team that connected all the important trade routes. There was a common and prevalent trade language—Koine Greek—in which Paul could communicate with people from other lands even when he didn't know their native tongues or have a translator available. The shipping routes were established, with many ships from around the Empire constantly arriving to and leaving from almost every port of the Mediterranean Sea. Jewish synagogues and communities, established in most cities, presented him with ready-made beachheads for most of his missionary endeavors.

In his Jewish family, which could trace its history to the tribe of Benjamin (Philippians 3:4–6), Paul was steeped in the Torah from his earliest days (Deuteronomy 6:1–10). His lineage was very important to his parents, for they raised their son to be a highly committed man of faith, fluent in Mosaic Law and knowledgeable about the prophets and writings of the Old Testament. It is unlikely that they were Jewish in name only or mere cultural Israelites; more probably they were very dedicated to their heritage. Paul said he had been "circumcised the eighth day, of the nation of Israel, of the tribe of Benjamin." He referred to himself as a "Hebrew of Hebrews" and "as to the Law, a Pharisee" (Philippians 3:4–6).

His parents gave him the name of the most famous leader of the tribe of Benjamin who became the first king of Israel, Saul. Unlike Saul, who reigned selfishly and corruptly over Israel for 40 years, Paul would be the epitome of one sold out for a cause greater than himself, first for the defense of Israel but ultimately for the person of Jesus.

Paul's family was probably committed to the Pharisaical expression of Judaism, which means that they would have placed great emphasis on observing both Mosaic Law and the oral Torah, which was a set of teachings that would be written down much later and called the Talmud. Paul would have been trained from his earliest days to view life from the perspective of this strict sect and to evaluate things as clean or unclean, pure or impure, good or bad. This mind-set developed into an all-or-nothing personality which exhibited itself throughout Paul's life, whether he was hunting down Christians to arrest them or himself standing trial before the emperor for his own faith in Jesus Christ.[1]

Most scholars assume that because Paul held Roman citizenship, he came from a wealthy family. As Acts 22:28 tells us, Roman citizenship was expensive, and Paul's was passed along to him by virtue of his birth. Even if his family had been given Roman citizenship earlier for another reason, such as heroic service to the emperor, it nevertheless provided Paul's family with opportunities that could elevate their status and their standard of living. It was also very valuable to Paul during his travels throughout the Empire. As a Roman citizen, he could not be punished without a fair trial, and any arrests had to follow a certain legal protocol, which required that he be treated with greater respect. His citizenship seems never to have prevented his arrest, but it did make the arrests more tolerable at times and even gave him, finally, the opportunity to go to Rome to stand before Caesar. He used these privileges a few times over the course of his journeys (Acts 16:37; 22:25; 25:16).

Unlike many Christian leaders today whose salaries allow them to devote themselves to ministry, all good Pharisaic scholars and teachers had to earn their livelihoods by acquiring and practicing a trade. It is likely that Paul learned his trade as a tentmaker from his father, as was customary in those days. Whenever the need arose, he could make a living plying his trade, a useful one in every part of the Roman Empire.

Having grown up in a Roman city and then gone to study in Jerusalem, Paul learned several languages. He spoke Greek fluently and could perhaps read and understand some Latin as well. Because of his parents' religious devotion, he likely spoke Aramaic at home, although Greek often became the native language among the Jewish Diaspora. As Jesus' first words to him were in Aramaic, it is a safe assumption that it was Paul's heart language. Given his strict training in Jerusalem, he would also have learned Hebrew (Acts 22:2; Philippians 3:5). God's sovereign hand is evident, for Paul would later demonstrate an aptitude for learning languages and would write eloquently in Koine Greek, the predominant language of his day.

Some writers make much of the fact that Tarsus, a city that was a thousand years old by the time of Paul's birth, was a center for culture, with schools that were devoted to philosophy, rhetoric, and law. This may have greatly influenced Paul, but that more likely occurred when he lived there as an adult rather than during his youth, when I believe he would have been sequestered from such influence by his devout Jewish home. There is no doubt, however, that the influence of the culture around him helped to prepare him for his call to the Gentiles after his conversion.

In some ways, Paul was what we today would call a "third culture kid"—not fully Jewish and not fully Roman but having a third culture made up of both. Even though his family would have been committed to life in a separate Jewish subculture, he was still immersed in a leading Roman city and was affected by that experience. If he had been born and raised only in Israel, he could easily have known only Jewish culture, which would have made him less able to adapt to and learn other cultures and languages. But because of his upbringing in Tarsus, he had many advantages for the work he would ultimately set out to accomplish. He could be at home everywhere he went and yet not feel the need to stay, because he never truly fit in anywhere.

As a Jew growing up far from Jerusalem, he probably came to see that his religious beliefs were not bound by geography. Once he came to see Jesus as the Way, all that he had once learned from Jewish law and teaching began to take on far greater significance. In a sense, he was being educated into his destiny before he could possibly have understood its significance or the full depth of its truth.

It is possible that his family made the pilgrimage to Jerusalem on rare occasions for religious holy days. Such travels may have begun the pattern that would govern all of Paul's life—taking spiritual journeys for his faith in God.

It has been commonly assumed that at some point Saul of Tarsus was married and had at least one child. A good Pharisee always married and had a family; that was the expectation for such a role. But if he did have a family, it is not known what became of his wife and child, since neither

Paul nor Luke mentions either. There is much room for speculation but none for factual assertion. We cannot know, but Paul decided to remain single when he became a Christian. He even seems to imply that he had a gift for remaining celibate (1 Corinthians 7:7–8). Paul said, "Are you bound to a wife? Do not seek to be released. Are you released from a wife? Do not seek a wife" (1 Corinthians 7:27). He concedes that it would not be wrong to marry but that the person who marries loses some of the focus on mission that comes with not being bound in marriage (1 Corinthians 7:32–35). He also mentions that other apostles had the right to take their wives with them on their journeys but that he and Barnabas chose not to (1 Corinthians 9:5–6). We can conclude from these passages that he was single at the time of his conversion and remained so.

At some point in his young life (Acts 22:3; 26:4), Saul moved to Jerusalem and was trained to be a Pharisee. His enthusiasm must have been evident because the great Gamaliel, a respected Pharisee and teacher of Jewish law, chose to mentor him. Gamaliel's exceptional wisdom and respected status among his peers is demonstrated in that passage in Acts where he advises the Sanhedrin, in the church's early days, not to execute the apostles (Acts 5:33–42). He warns them that if the apostles' message is only of human origin, it will die all on its own, but if it is of God, it will not be stopped. Resisting it, he tells them, may even be fighting against God Himself. Paul later uses Gamaliel's name to gain some respect in a very tenuous situation (Acts 22:3).

Ideally, every believer needs to have mentors and to mentor others. Later, as we shall see, Barnabas also became a mentor to Paul. He was blessed to have good mentors, and he would grow to become one himself.

Your Story: Lessons from the Early Days that Mark our Destiny

It can be hard to believe in destiny. Surrendering to the idea that there is a master design for our life—one that we are meant to step into—can be a pill that is hard to swallow. It doesn't matter whether we come from a charmed childhood or from one full of deep scars and bitter memories, the concept of destiny is still a challenge. The idea of a personal fate threatens the hopeful future that some people carry with them every day— after all, a fated life may end up being very different from the life they dream of. For others, the thought that their destiny is foreordained is troubling because it means that a personal God may have arranged for them to be born into painful circumstances. Still others may just want to maintain the illusion of control. But whether we choose to accept the idea of destiny or not has no real bearing on its veracity. God has a unique calling for our life. Paul wrote to the believers at Ephesus:

> For we are His workmanship, created in Christ Jesus for good works, which God prepared beforehand so that we would walk in them. (Ephesians 2:10)

This was not a new concept in Jewish thought. In the Old Testament, King David wrote to God:

> Your eyes have seen my unformed substance;
> And in Your book were all written
> The days that were ordained for me,
> When as yet there was not one of them. (Psalm 139:16)

It is not within the scope of this book to address the eternal question of how our own free will works within the sovereignty of God, so I will not even attempt it. But when I say that you have a destiny, I mean that God has advance knowledge of your entire life, from your unique DNA to the desired hopes and longings of your soul. He loves you enough to die for you, and He wants you to be fulfilled in a uniquely designed calling He has selected specifically for you. He will not take away the gift He has given to you, but neither will He force it on you. His love for you is not the whole picture, however. He also wants you to love and trust Him because that, and really that alone, is the foundation of fulfilling God's calling for you. Therefore, it is essential that you have a choice in life, for love and trust are always a choice. If the choice is removed, so is the love. If you have no choice, you have no trust and you cannot love.

All of us are born for a reason, and in a time and place of God's choosing (Acts 17:24-28). Your parents may not have planned for you to come when you did, but you are no accident. If you have the right lenses, you may also see that you were born to a destiny that is better than you ever dreamed. The evidence may be all around you, waiting to be discovered. This destiny is not simply about a job or career. It is a call to follow Jesus into the depth of purpose He has ordained for your life, whatever vocation He uses to get you there. His Kingdom call transcends occupations and job descriptions. In fact, the call is not just about you. It is about Him and His purposes—He is not some high-in-the-sky career counselor with a wonderful plan for your own personal life. You will not regret the plans He has forged for your life, but it is not all about your own personal happiness and fulfillment. The purpose of God on your life is much more than that. It is so valuable that even when your happiness and security are at stake, it is still worth the risk and the cost of surrendering to it. There are none who risk that come to regret it; there are many who do not whose lives are full of regret.

Discovering Your Destiny

God's fingerprints are on our early life, but most of us cannot see them until we look back. Steve Jobs once quipped, "You can't connect the dots looking forward; you can only connect them looking backwards. ... You have to trust that the dots will somehow connect in your future."[2]

J. Robert Clinton refers to this young phase of our lives as our "sovereign foundations." We really do not have control over the factors that shape us at this stage of development, any more than we can choose our parents, birthplace, or birthday.

As you continue to grow, you can look back at this stage of development, and perhaps recognize that all the factors of your early life were sovereignly designed for a purpose and contributed toward fulfilling your calling. You can piece together some of the destiny you were prepared to walk into, and maybe you can even start to make sense of your childhood. God can bring healing, redemption, and meaning to the hardships you have experienced, as difficult as that is to believe. He is not the author of evil or a stranger to suffering. He is big enough to use even the consequences of evil for His own purpose (Proverbs 16:4), all with grace and compassion.

Winston Churchill once said, "It is a mistake to try to look too far ahead. The chain of destiny can only be grasped one link at a time."[3] I hope that as you grasp each link of your destiny, you will be able to make more sense of what has occurred in your life and even of some of what is coming your way.

Just as Paul's early background doesn't come close to revealing what God would do with him, analysis of your own early life will not reveal your full destiny. It can help, however, to consider some of the ways God can redeem the pain of your life and use that as well as His blessings for His purposes.

 **Early Life Reflections**

Many of us have not recognized the hand of God in our birth and early years. For the purposes of this book, I simply want you to consider that God may have a reason why your early life was the way it was, and I want to give you the hope of discovering a redemptive purpose. Finding God's hand at work in our earlier life can help us put to rest some of the issues of our past, can bring some healing to wounds hindering us in the present, and can also help us to discover a destined purpose for our future.

You can begin by doing an inventory of your early life and taking stock of the factors that influenced you to become the person you are today. This is a healthy way to balance your past and focus your present. Pray and ask God to help you in this process. Here are some helpful questions to prayerfully ask:

- Why was I born at the time and in the place that God selected for me?
- What is special about the cultural soil that I emerged from and that I carry with me in every thought and impulse?
- For what purpose might God use the kinds of things that make me excited or sad?
- What unique and positive traits might come from the childhood I had?

Here are some other factors to consider as you look back over your early life. Go over each one and make notes on what may have been an important influence in making you the person you are today:

- Family heritage and relatives
- Repeated behavior patterns passed down generationally
- Friends and associates

- Geopolitical and historical events surrounding that time of your life
- Personality traits
- Birth order and siblings
- Cultural inclinations
- Language and education
- Painful and positive memories
- Passions and preferences
- Strengths and weaknesses
- Abilities and vulnerabilities

Next, learn to respond positively to God's purposes and His leading you through your past experiences. To move forward into the destiny God has for you, being at peace with your past will be essential. Forgive those who hurt you, not for their sake but your own. Even if you don't want to forgive people for the evil they have committed, you cannot move forward without setting yourself free from people in your past. You may not feel like letting them off the hook, but if you do not forgive them, you keep yourself bound to your past, rather than moving forward into your destined future. At the risk of stating the obvious, forgiveness is not for those who deserve it but for those who do not. Forgiveness is always substitutionary—it means accepting the evil done to you and releasing any demand for payment. Jesus forgave us, and to walk in His love, we must also forgive others and leave justice to God.[4] Make a list of the people who hurt you throughout your life. Then go down the list one at a time and state out loud for each: "Lord, I forgive_____, for the _____ done to me. Please set me free from the wounds and bondage caused by this pain. I choose to leave all justice in your hands."

It is not just the negative events of your past that you must reconcile. Some people are still living in the memories of their past accomplishments. Some people are enslaved to the past because of the glory days and some because of the gory ones. Paul balanced his past and his present by always pursuing a better future—a future of knowing Christ more fully.

In Philippians 3, Paul lists much of his background, only to say that "forgetting what lies behind and reaching forward to what lies ahead, I press on toward the goal for the prize of the upward call of God in Christ Jesus" (Philippians 3:13–14). Think of the simple exercises in this chapter as merely looking in the rearview mirror as you face forward, pressing on in your pursuit of Jesus' calling for your life. Paul used his past to identify with his mission field (Acts 22:1–21), to confirm his unique calling in life (Galatians 1:11–24), to demonstrate the radical transformation of his life (1 Timothy 1:14–16), and to motivate himself for his zealous commitment in the present (1 Corinthians 15:8–11; Ephesians 2:1–13). He never saw his past as an excuse for fruitless living in the present.

After you have made a list of the influential events, people, and qualities of your childhood, try to place them into the same types of useful categories that Paul himself used. Ask yourself, *How have these events, people, or qualities helped me to . . .*

- Identify with a specific mission? In what ways have these factors prepared me to help a certain type of person?
- Confirm my unique calling in life? What are the fingerprints of God that shaped me for what He is now calling me to do?
- Perceive God's redemptive love and power? How have these factors told the story of God's love and power in my life?
- Motivate myself for greater service in the present? How have these events, people, and qualities from my past fueled my love and passion for Jesus in the present?

There is a great deal more for you to discover in addition to what you can find in your early years. That period of your life is just the beginning. In the next chapter, we will look at the important developmental phase of inner-life growth. When we do, we will see that a man named Saul had, unknown to himself, a very important and consequential divine appointment on a certain road to Damascus.

CHAPTER 2

NEW LIFE

A Sharp Detour onto a Straight Street

> *A person often meets his destiny on the road he took to avoid it.*
> — Jean de La Fontaine

> *And last of all, as to one untimely born, He appeared to me also. For I am the least of the apostles, and not fit to be called an apostle, because I persecuted the church of God. But by the grace of God I am what I am, and His grace toward me did not prove vain.*
> —The apostle Paul (1 Corinthians 15:8–10)

Do you ever pause in a routine morning and wonder if this day will alter your life forever? Probably not, but I must confess that I sometimes do. The truth is that life-altering days often hit us when we least expect them. We easily get lulled into a lack of anticipation by the succession of so many days that do not make much of a difference. Then, without warning—BANG—something hits us and changes us for all the days that follow.

One day the Pharisee named Saul of Tarsus was on a road trip heading to Damascus from Jerusalem to arrest and contain the new sect of people who believed Jesus to be the Christ, the Anointed One, the Messiah. Saul's day on this life-changing trip likely began in normal fashion, without any indication that everything was about to change forever. We live life only by journeying forward, blind to and unaware of the "Damascus Road" episodes that are coming our way.

Paul's Story: Conversion and New Life

In the first mention of Saul, later called Paul, we are introduced to him as an approving witness of the execution of a great man of God named Stephen. As dark as the story is, it marks the starting point for Saul's dramatic transformation, and for that reason alone it remains a pivotal account in the book of Acts. Saul always regretted his role in the execution, but in Acts 22, he bravely includes that shameful event in his testimony to the Jews because it was such an important marker for the rest of his life.

We do not know where Saul was coming from or going to when he became involved in Stephen's death. We do know from the spontaneity of the account in Acts 6 and 7 that Stephen's stoning was not an item on Saul's to-do list or an appointment in his planner for that day. In God's providence, he took a detour from whatever he was supposed to be doing and became immersed in Stephen's trial and immediate execution.

Stoning Stephen was Executing Jesus…Again

Luke describes Stephen and his execution with specific language and detail. It is strange that the martyrdom of the apostle James, one of the Twelve personally chosen and trained by Jesus, is given just one sentence (Acts 12:2), whereas the account of Stephen's death is given two chapters. I believe a primary reason for the lengthy description of this incident in Paul's story is that this event is the first domino to fall, initiating the momentum of everything yet to come in the book of Acts. This day would not just end one man's life and change another's—it would also change human history because of the effect it would have on Paul's life. Thus, Luke gives us all the details, probably as recounted by Paul himself.

One of the ways Luke emphasizes the importance of the story is by portraying Stephen as Christlike. In a real sense, as Saul endorses the execution of Stephen, he is also executing Jesus. Later, when Saul falls to the ground on the road to Damascus and is confronted by Jesus in all His glory, the risen Lord asks Saul, "Why are you persecuting *ME?*" (emphasis added). He then identifies Himself as "Jesus whom you are persecuting." Apparently, it is not only Luke who recognizes the connection between Stephen's death and Christ's; Jesus Himself sees it that way. Jesus feels all the pain and humiliation that we encounter for our faith. Even if we are executed for our belief, we are never alone, for Jesus is with us in that moment feeling every bullet, blade, rock, nail or noose.

Stephen was indeed an embodiment of Christ in his work, as well as in his trial and execution. You can actually find depictions of Stephen's execution described in almost the same language by the same human author, Luke, in his own gospel account. Here are some ways Luke goes out of his way to emphasize that Stephen is a mirror image of Jesus. Among the people, he performed wonders and miracles that drew crowds to hear his message (Acts 6:8; Luke 7:22). His opponents failed miserably to refute him in argument (Acts 6:10; Luke 13:17; 20:1-8, 27-40). Those same opponents brought Stephen to the Sanhedrin without cause. As they had done with Jesus, they stirred up false witnesses to testify against him (Acts 6:11–13; Luke 23:2). The accusation against Stephen was the same as that leveled at Jesus—that He would destroy the temple (Acts 6:13–14; Luke 21:6). Jesus and Stephen were both brought before Caiaphas, the high priest who served until AD 36, as well as the Sanhedrin. After a long and passionate speech explaining why Israel's history pointed to Jesus, Stephen told them that the temple was not fit for God to live in, and that God is bigger than any building made with human hands. He then, like Jesus, pronounced judgment on his accusers, saying that, despite their words to the contrary, they were just like their forefathers, who murdered the prophets whom God had sent (Acts 7:51-53; Luke 11:47-51).

When Jesus was before the same seat of judgment, His accusers asked Him if He was indeed the Messiah. He answered, "…and you shall see the Son of Man sitting at the right hand of power, and coming with the clouds of heaven" (Mark 14:62; Luke 22:69). And Stephen gazed up from the same seat, likely before the same officials, and stated, "Behold, I see the heavens opened up and the Son of Man standing at the right hand of God" (Acts 7:56). The words of Jesus, which cemented His own execution, were now being thrown back into the faces of the same accusers. They had to either admit that they were wrong and confess to killing the Messiah or execute this other man. Without delay and without proper protocol, Stephen was driven outside the city gates by a yelling mob and stoned to death. He called out, "Lord Jesus, receive my spirit," mirroring

Jesus' words on the cross to God the Father, "FATHER, INTO YOUR HANDS I COMMIT MY SPIRIT" (Luke 23:46). Like Jesus, as Stephen was dying, he prayed that God would not hold this sin against his executioners (Acts 7:60; see also Luke 23:34). The Holy Spirit, through Luke, was most certainly painting Stephen as a representative of Jesus so that Saul would come to know that he was not just executing this disciple, but Jesus Himself…again. In a real sense, all of us are guilty of the execution of Christ, because He died to carry our guilt and shame so that we could be set free and join God's family. Saul of Tarsus would discover this truth personally and ultimately carry that knowledge throughout his life. We should do the same.

By God's providence, Saul of Tarsus was drawn that day to the public spectacle of Stephen being confronted by the Council of the Sanhedrin. As things continued to unfold, "they began stoning him; and the witnesses laid aside their robes at the feet of a young man named Saul" (Acts 7:58). Luke then recorded, "Saul was in hearty agreement with putting him to death" (Acts 8:1). That moment would launch Saul on a mission to stamp out the followers of Jesus. "Saul began ravaging the church, entering house after house, and dragging off men and women, he would put them in prison" (Acts 8:3). The older leaders of the Sanhedrin were in favor of Saul's enthusiastic agenda, and they let him run with a long leash (Acts 26:9–11).

What happened next is one of the great ironies of Scripture. In Acts 1:8, Jesus had said to the Twelve, "You will receive power when the Holy Spirit has come upon you; and you shall be My witnesses both in Jerusalem, and in all Judea and Samaria, and even to the remotest part of the earth" (Acts 1:8). But it took this persecution, instigated by Saul, to send the people of God out into all of Judea and Samaria. Acts 8:1 says that all the believers in the church were scattered by this persecution and left Jerusalem—except the "sent ones" (the apostles).

Don't miss the sarcasm here simply because the translators have used the word *apostles*. Anyone who read and spoke Greek would have immediately caught it. The ones who were "sent" were the only ones who didn't go.[1] Until this moment everyone stayed in Jerusalem, and none ventured to spread the good news into the regions beyond. Because of Saul's persecution, the early church finally scattered into the very fields Jesus had commanded them to visit.

Thus, even as Saul in zealous rage attempted to stamp out Christianity, he still had more to do with getting the saints mobilized to spread the Kingdom of God than all twelve Jerusalem apostles combined.

I do not for a moment think that those apostles were deliberately disobedient. I simply think that they lacked the full faith and understanding that would have allowed them to go. Perhaps they were bound by what they felt were their responsibilities of leadership and by an inherited prejudice against Samaritans and Gentiles that they couldn't recognize within themselves. It is entirely possible that they felt their faith needed the temple and Jerusalem for validity. They probably even believed it noble to remain in the heat of persecution. For whatever reason, they failed to obey Jesus' command to go and be His witnesses.

Instead, God used Saul to mobilize His people into His mission beyond Jerusalem to Judea and Samaria. The Lord would then use Saul's redeemed life—his life as Paul—to extend His Kingdom "to the ends of the earth." Even before Saul was redeemed and regenerated, he had more to do with spreading the good news of Jesus to the world than any other person.

A Divine Appointment

There is one missionary journey that we won't find pictured in the maps at the back of our Bible. On this journey, a man named Saul was heading to Damascus. His mission was not to spread the news about Jesus but to stop others from doing so. He was going not to make disciples but to arrest and imprison them. It was on this path that Saul experienced something that brought radical change to every moment of the rest of his life.

In Acts 9, Luke said that Saul of Tarsus was "still breathing threats and murder against the disciples of the Lord." Saul requested documents from the Sanhedrin to authorize him to extend the persecution and follow the Christians who had scattered to other parts of the world. He wanted to go after those in Damascus, but we can easily imagine Saul making more than one such journey.

Later in his life, Paul described this time: "And as I punished them often in all the synagogues, I tried to force them to blaspheme; and being furiously enraged at them, I kept pursuing them *even to foreign cities*" (Acts 26:11; emphasis added). Even before he began following the Way, he was inclined to go on journeys on behalf of his spiritual convictions, twisted as they were.

The conversion of Saul is perhaps one of the most crucial stories in the book of Acts, indeed in all of history.[2] Luke told this story once in the chronological narrative (Acts 9:1–31) and then twice more (Acts 22:1–21; 26:2–23) as he quoted Paul retelling it. I've drawn information from all three accounts in my explanations within this chapter.

Saul and his companions were traveling in the heat of the day and nearing Damascus when a light brighter than the sun suddenly burst upon them. That the light of heaven shone brighter than the midday sun shows us how incredibly radiant the Lord is. His presence caused everything, even the sunlight, to fade into the background. Saul's companions could see the light, but they could not see the Lord or understand His voice. Saul, however, could both see and hear the Lord. Falling to his knees, Saul heard the voice say: "Saul, Saul, why are you persecuting Me? It is hard for you to kick against the goads."[3] Whatever spiritual prodding Saul may already have received, until this moment he had rejected it all and proceeded with determination, fully believing that he had been fulfilling God's will. But finally, when Jesus revealed Himself, He got Saul to pay attention.

The Holy Spirit pursues those who are the objects of our Lord's love, even if they fail to recognize it. When Jesus wants to, He has ways of getting our attention. Usually that involves asking questions. When addressing someone who has been particularly foolish, He will begin the question with the personal name of the one He is addressing—saying it twice, to really get the needed attention. I refer to this as the heavenly echo, and we hear it in "Simon, Simon" (Luke 22:31), "Martha, Martha" (Luke 10:41), even "Jerusalem, Jerusalem" (Luke 13:34). I often imagine Him slowly shaking His head when I have been particularly foolish, and in my mind, I hear Him sigh, "Neil, Neil."

In Luke's story we also hear the heavenly echo: "Saul, Saul" (Acts 9:4). There is not going to be any way for this Pharisee to ignore the Lord's guidance at this point. In addition to showing him the blinding light and speaking to him in a loud voice, the risen Christ gets Saul's attention by addressing him in Aramaic (Acts 26:14), something we cannot recognize in our English translations. Jesus identified Himself to Saul as the one whom he was persecuting. Gamaliel, his mentor, was right after all. Saul was indeed fighting against the Lord (Acts 5:33-39).

Jesus then told Saul to continue to Damascus, where he would receive instructions concerning all he had been appointed to do. When Saul rose from the ground, he was blind. What a contrast—from seeing a light brighter than the sun to stumbling in darkness! One moment he was able to see but was spiritually blind, then he was physically blind but could see spiritually for the first time.

Saul's companions helped him get to the city, and they stayed in a house on a street called Straight owned by a man named Judas. Saul stayed there for three days, still blind, without eating or drinking.

Imagine what must have been going on in Saul's head after he encountered Jesus, on the heels of overseeing the deaths and imprisonment of several of His people (Acts 26:10). His entire life and all he had lived for was turned upside down, and the Lord gave him three solid days to let this sink in. So, he sat waiting and wondering, listening and praying, and all the time fasting.

During those dark days, Saul received a vision that a man named Ananias would come and heal him of his blindness.[4] God shows mercy even in—or perhaps especially in—our darkest moments. When Paul's eyes no longer could see, and he was full of regret for his stubborn blindness all the time that he could see, what would be the best way for God to show His mercy? In an ironic blessing, Saul's darkness was invaded—by a *vision.* God's mercy is everlasting and always amazing. The vision was also a promise that these dark days had an end. While perhaps the first part of those three days was full of sorrow and tears, I think the latter part was full of joy and worship.

Like Jesus in the tomb for three days before He was raised, Saul spent three days in darkness awaiting his new life. Eventually a powerful confirmation of Saul's new calling came to him and permanently removed all doubt. Saul heard his name spoken once again in Aramaic, only this time it was not repeated in disapproval but coupled with the endearing term "brother." Ananias came to him, laid his hands on him, and said, "Brother Saul, the Lord Jesus, who appeared to you on the road by which you were coming, has sent me so that you may regain your sight and be filled with the Holy Spirit." Immediately the scales fell from Saul's eyes, and he could see again. We later learn (Galatians 1:1) that he also received a prophetic word from the Lord that would reveal a life calling. Try to imagine the gravity of this moment—not only was Jesus not Saul's avowed enemy, He also had a plan for Saul. And the plan was incredible. In Acts 22:14-16, Luke quoted Paul recounting the words spoken to him by Ananias: "The God of our fathers has appointed you to know His will and to see the Righteous One and to hear an utterance from His mouth. For you will be a witness for Him to all men of what you have seen and heard. Now why do you delay? Get up and be baptized, and wash away your sins, calling on His name."

The prophetic word, the healing, and the mercy and forgiveness Saul had received must have renewed his body. Immediately Saul arose and was baptized. I feel it is significant that the great apostle Paul was baptized by a man barely known in the Scriptures. Ananias, a faithful but common man, was chosen as the Lord's vessel to restore Saul, heal him, baptize him, and announce his new calling. There was not a laying on of hands by any of the Twelve. Jesus came to Saul through the hands of a simple man otherwise unknown in history. That's the point. It is the presence of Jesus that makes any of us special for His service, whether we are one of the Twelve, Ananias, Saul, or just ourselves.

No matter how dramatic your calling is when Jesus speaks to you, confirmation from a secondary source is always appreciated. Jesus doesn't mind confirming such things because they are important to remember for the rest of your life, and He does know how easily we can be deceived. Saul's doubts and fears were laid to rest when a man he had never met called him "Brother." One moment he may have been wondering if he would ever know what was going on. The next moment, a man clearly directed by the Lord arrived where Saul was staying. The man somehow knew what Saul had seen and heard from the Lord on the road coming into town. The man's name was the same as that of the man Saul had seen come to him in a vision. Then, to establish once and for all that this was from God, the man laid hands on Saul and healed his blindness. Finally, after all this dramatic confirmation, Ananias told Saul his destiny and gave him his new orders from the Lord. Those orders, substantiated in so many ways, would carry the man through many dark moments and horrific trials in the future. God is faithful to His word.

New Life

Paul didn't wait to pursue his new calling. He showed up at the same synagogue where he was supposed to go, but his authority and his orders had changed radically. What a surprise for those who had come expecting to see the notorious Saul of Tarsus, enemy of the Way (Acts 9:13; 26:11). Instead, they heard the same man affirming that Jesus is the Son of God. Paul got busy fast, serving the church with the same determination and zeal he formerly used to persecute it. He stayed some time in Damascus, preaching in the synagogues, and he likely traveled through Arabia during this season while maintaining Damascus as his base (Galatians 1:17).

Many people speculate that Paul went off to Arabia to be alone with God and have his theology straightened out. Personally, I find that hard to believe, knowing the passionate determination of this man who was now in his mid-thirties. He was told that he would preach the gospel, and I believe that is what he set out to do. Right from the start, he "kept increasing in strength and confounding the Jews who lived at Damascus by proving that this Jesus is the Christ" (Acts 9:22). I believe that he worked out his new faith in the best possible place—not in Arabia, but in obedience, doing the work God called him to.

Isolation and reflection were an important part of Paul's development, no doubt, but I imagine that he would not have volunteered for such a respite, especially at such a young age and at this early stage. The time of being alone and listening was to come, but as is the case for most of us, it had to be forced on him by the removal of all other options.

Rejection in Arabia, Damascus, and Jerusalem

We don't know exactly what Paul was doing in Damascus and Arabia, but he got the Gentile authorities upset, and I can hardly imagine that quietly sitting on a rock in the desert listening to God would have done that. According to his own recounting, the ethnarch under Aretas IV, king of the Nabataeans (Arabia), was guarding the city gates of Damascus to try to capture Paul and kill him. Luke writes that it was the Jews who may have stirred up this persecution, probably by instigating some sort of unrest, which set the Gentile law enforcers of the land after Paul. But Paul found out.

In a dramatic escape, Paul was let down in a basket through a window in the wall of the city to sneak away under cover of night. It is possible that this was three years into his new faith (Galatians 1:18), and that he was already a "basket case." His newfound faith, adrenaline, youthful passion, and naiveté could take him only so far. He was being chased out of town for the first time—but certainly not the last.

Once again, Paul was on the Damascus Road but this time heading in the opposite direction—and not under the midday sun but a canopy of stars. I wonder how long he paused over the spot on that road where his new life had begun. It was close to the city where he was a wanted man, and so perhaps even under cover of night he didn't have time to reflect on what he possibly viewed as a kind of holy ground—a location that held a special but haunting place in his heart.

Having offended not only the Jews but also the Gentiles that he had been called to reach, Paul returned to Jerusalem to get to know the spiritual fathers of the church. If he was not welcomed in Damascus and Arabia, imagine how cold his reception must have been in Jerusalem. Those who were once his friends were now his enemies, and those who were once his enemies could hardly be friendly after all he had done to them and their community.

Paul tried to establish fellowship with the disciples, but they were afraid and wanted nothing to do with him. His old associates were probably even less welcoming. It was at that moment, when all seemed to turn their backs on him, that he met a friend who would leave a lasting mark on his life. His name was Barnabas. I like the way the New American Standard Bible says it: "But Barnabas *took hold of him* and brought him to the apostles and described to them how he had seen the Lord on the road, and that He had talked to him, and how at Damascus he had spoken out boldly in the name of Jesus" (Acts 9:27, emphasis added).

When Saul was blind in Damascus, Ananias had come and laid hands on him with a message of hope. In Jerusalem, when he was again in difficulty, another new friend laid hands on him and welcomed him. There is nothing quite like the warm touch of a friend in a lonely situation. Barnabas, as described in Acts, seemed uniquely gifted to see the potential in people's souls. He also seemed to know exactly what they needed, and he loved to lift their spirits and draw out the good things he saw in them. This quality was such a part of his life that the people of the Jerusalem church had changed his name from Joseph to Barnabas, which literally means "Son of Encouragement" (Acts 4:36).

After Barnabas's intervention, Paul spoke with Peter and James and set out to begin his new ministry in Jerusalem. There was only one place he could go to start this new work—the synagogue where Stephen had once preached. Paul may have felt bound to reconcile his past mistakes as quickly as he could, and so he took up the work of the man he had helped to kill, witnessing to the Hellenistic Jews as Stephen had done.

What seemed like a wonderful plan, however, quickly crashed and burned. In little more than two weeks (Galatians 1:18), Paul was once again on a journey. Since he was seen as a traitor, his work among the Hellenistic Jews was even less well received than Stephen's had been (Acts 9:29). The Lord appeared to Paul while he was in the temple and said, "Make haste, and get out of Jerusalem quickly, because they will not accept your testimony about Me" (Acts 22:18). When the Lord said, "Make haste" and "quickly" in the same sentence, I suspect it meant "Head for the door now, and don't pack any bags!" But Paul tried to convince the Lord of his own usefulness in Jerusalem. It may well be that he was hoping that if he stayed, he would have a chance to make up for what he had done to Stephen. This wasn't an argument he would win. The Lord said to him, emphatically, "Go! For I will send you far away to the Gentiles." In other words, "Your calling is Mine to decide, and you are not called to reconcile your past. I already did that. Get moving!"

I always chuckle when I see the beauty of how God decides people's destinies. Matthew, the hated tax collector who was considered a traitor to his people because of his cooperation with the oppressive Gentile Roman government, was chosen to write the account recorded in his

Gospel for the Jews. Most of us, apparently including Paul, would have thought that the Pharisees were better prepared to preach to the Jews instead of a despised tax collector. Then God chose Paul, a strict, well-educated, and very Jewish Pharisee, to be His apostle to communicate the gospel to the Gentiles. Jesus sees things very differently than we humans do and so said to Paul, "I will send you away *to the Gentiles*." In Christ, the things that once were considered our greatest strengths become our weaknesses, and the things that we once considered weaknesses are turned into strengths. In all of this, it is the power and presence of Jesus that makes the difference, not our own education, experience, or excellence.

Benched in Tarsus

The disciples sent Paul from Jerusalem to Caesarea, then on to Tarsus. He had been rejected in Damascus, and now he had also been rejected in Jerusalem. All he could do was head home to Tarsus, where he would spend the next ten years. He may have felt deeply discouraged, the way any great athlete does when he is sent to the bench while the game is still being played.

There is no mention in the Bible of Paul's family except that he had a sister and nephew (Acts 23:16) and a woman who was like an adopted mother (Romans 16:13). So, what was waiting for him when he returned home?

As Jesus once commented, a prophet's hometown and own people are usually the most resistant to his or her message (Luke 4:24). That was likely the case here as well, since that seems to be a way to account for the five times Paul was scourged by the Jews before he wrote 2 Corinthians in AD 56. I am sure Paul preached the gospel any chance he got, and he may even have started churches (Galatians 1:21; Acts 15:23, 41), but to stay an entire decade in one place would have been a long time for this "sent one." Many speculate that it was in Arabia that Paul sat and listened to the Lord about the important things concerning his life and faith (Galatians 1:11–12), but I believe it was while he was sidelined in Tarsus that Jesus personally tutored him and prepared him to fulfill his destiny.

Tarsus was a good place to be stationed if he was to learn how to evangelize the Gentiles because it was a renowned cultural center for law, philosophy, and rhetoric. There would be days to come when Paul would pour out all that he had bottled up within himself, but these days in Tarsus were about receiving necessary lessons. In this town where he had once learned languages, his sacred heritage as one of God's chosen people, and the Jewish holy writings, he now learned pagan culture, philosophy, and rhetorical skills, which would serve him well in his future journeys. He may have intuitively picked up a lot as a child in this town, but during this decade he was a highly motivated student in a university town because now he had been called by Jesus to reach the Gentile world.

His education in Tarsus paid dividends in his future work. In his epistles, Paul would quote Menander and the Cretan poet Epimenides. In his speech to the stoic philosophers in Athens, he used apt allusions to Aeschylus's *Eumenides* and to Plato's *Phaedo*, and he made a tactful paraphrase of Plato's *Republic*.[5] His quote "For we also are His children," in that message on Mars Hill (Acts 17:28) is an allusion to Aratus's *Phenomena*.[6]

While those ten years in Tarsus are a glaring hole in Paul's story, we can assume a few things to fill in some of the gaps. When he wrote 2 Corinthians in AD 56, Paul recounted many of the sufferings he endured for the sake of Christ, the majority of which do not appear in Acts; perhaps some of them occurred during this ten-year sojourn in his hometown and the surrounding area.

In that letter, Paul says that he received thirty-nine lashes from the Jews on five different occasions.[7] The concept of administering thirty-nine lashes was to punish a man by bringing him right to the edge of death without killing him. None of these instances was recorded in Acts, and so we may assume that some, if not all, occurred during those ten years. He was brought to the point of death in this manner *five times*. He would later write to the Galatians in the earliest of his letters: "I bear on my body the brand-marks of Jesus" (Galatians 6:17). It is unfathomable how someone could endure this severe pain even once, let alone five times. What could possibly compel Paul to bear such suffering?

This type of scourging was sometimes meant to purge and restore a brother to the synagogue instead of excommunicating him. The punishment was executed by three or more leaders called the *bet din*, or house of judges, and was exercised for a number of reasons given in the Mishnah (a collection of oral laws and traditions of the second temple Jews that eventually would be written down after the New Testament was completed); Makkoth 3:1–9 lists several reasons for this punishment, including being a false teacher and entering the temple unclean, both of which Paul would be accused of having done simply by preaching the good news of Jesus.[8] Paul saw the synagogues as strategically important for the mission he was ultimately called to fulfill, and so perhaps he chose to be beaten raw in this way just to maintain his access. He could have escaped this horrendous anguish by being excommunicated or keeping his mouth shut, but neither was a real option for him, and so instead he endured.

There was a statement in the Jewish oral law (the Talmud) that if a sinner offended again after a previous beating, he was to suffer the same punishment a second time, heal, and then be scourged again for the third time.[9] Only after that would he be allowed back into the synagogue. After the transgressor is scourged twice in this way for his second offense, he is to be treated again as family and allowed access to the synagogue. Perhaps this is how Paul came to suffer so many of these punishments—all so that he could continue to preach the gospel to the people he loved so much.[10]

Paul later wrote to the Romans that he was willing to go much farther than this—that he would even go to hell for the sake of his countrymen. He said "I am telling the truth in Christ, I am not lying, my conscience testifies with me in the Holy Spirit, that I have great sorrow and unceasing grief in my heart. For I could wish that I myself were accursed, separated from Christ for the sake of my brethren, my kinsmen according to the flesh" (Romans 9:1–3). This love for people who would continue to punish him is not normal—it's not human, but divine. It is the love of Christ, who also endured lashes, wrath, and crucifixion for those who hated him.

Every time Paul preached the gospel in the synagogues, he knew full well the punishment he might have to endure—perhaps inflicted upon him by the very elders who had once taught him as a child. I imagine he weighed the cost and many times decided to preach anyway. He truly loved his enemies. It is very possible that he received a scourging for preaching the gospel, and then afterward preached again, and that he then received two more punishments, with some healing time in between. Then he preached the gospel yet again and forced the synagogue officials to order two more scourges for his heresy. From this we can see how much Paul loved the Jews and how much he was willing to go through for Jesus. We can also see how important access to the synagogue was to Paul's mission. Finally, this would also explain how he ended up receiving this form of punishment five times.

The account of Paul's life recorded by Luke in Acts plus additional information from Paul's epistles still leave us with significant gaps in the timeline. Somewhere in those unknown periods, Paul was shipwrecked three times and spent a night and a day floating in the ocean.[11] He received two additional beatings with rods during events not found in Acts (Luke records one of the three beating in Acts 16:22). All of this happened sometime before AD 56, when he wrote his second epistle to the Corinthians. It is likely that during these difficult days Paul kept trying to do the work and met disaster after disaster, all as preparation for the work that would come...eventually.

This was Paul's graduate school and his training for future deployment. Local legend says that he retreated into the hills of Tarsus to a cave where he received the special revelation of the third heaven mentioned in 2 Corinthians 12:1–10. This timing does match the timeframe presented in the passage. Regardless of when and where Paul received this revelation, there is no doubt that during those stressful and difficult years in Tarsus he was being taught by Jesus in person. He would say to the Galatians: "For I would have you know, brethren, that the gospel which was preached by me is not according to man. For I neither received it from man, nor was I taught it, but I received it through a revelation of Jesus Christ" (Galatians 1:11–12).

Compared to the exciting first three years of his Christian life, these ten years must have been full of suffering and rejection. We never really hear of great fruitfulness from these years, although there are reports of churches in this area a few years later (Acts 15:41). There would eventually be some lasting fruit from this period, but it appears that this time was more about getting character into Paul than getting competence out of him. Later, it took only ten years for Paul to establish self-sufficient reproducing church movements in five entire provinces of the Roman Empire—Galatia, Macedonia, Achaia, Asia, and Illyricum. In contrast, the work during this decade in Syria and Cilicia must have seemed slow and tedious indeed.

While Paul was "on the bench," the real game continued to play out. The gospel broke out among the Gentiles. First Peter was led by the Lord to share the gospel with Cornelius and his household (Acts 10–11). As word of that spread, a new church was started in Syrian Antioch (Acts 11:19–21). These Christians or "little Christs," as the locals called them, intentionally turned to the Gentiles to preach the gospel. To encourage this venture of faith and obedience, the Lord blessed the work with rapid and dramatic growth.

The apostles back in Jerusalem, hearing about this fast growth, sent the trusted leader Barnabas to scout out what was going on. Barnabas was truly excited and blessed by what he saw, but he soon left Antioch on a journey of his own. Barnabas remembered the young man he had found in Jerusalem and how God had called that man to preach the gospel to the Gentiles. He also remembered the man's short stint in Jerusalem and that he had been shipped out after only two weeks. Somehow, he knew in his heart that this was a perfect fit for Paul, and so, believing that God wanted Paul involved in Antioch, Barnabas went to Tarsus to call him back into action.

Luke says, "He left for Tarsus to look for Saul; and when he had found him, he brought him to Antioch" (Acts 11:25-26). We can only wonder how long Barnabas had to search for Paul. By this time Paul may have been traveling in the region preaching the gospel, floating in the sea after another shipwreck, or even in his cave, hearing from God. In any case, once he received this invitation from Barnabas, he did not delay in going to Antioch. When his name was called, he was ready to get back in the game.

In his early forties by now, Paul was better prepared for what lay ahead of him. That is not to say that Paul had learned all he needed to; as we will see, he still had much to learn. But it does mean that he had learned all he could in the classroom of Tarsus.

Back in the Game

Antioch, on the Orontes River sixteen miles from the Mediterranean, was at that time the third largest city in the Roman Empire. Only Rome and Alexandria were bigger. Together, Barnabas and Paul worked for a year serving this young and rapidly growing church. I imagine that there was a synergy among its members that can only be explained as the presence of Christ working through a small band of leaders completely devoted to Him.

The Jerusalem church seemed encumbered with a leadership team of twelve apostles, a group of elders (some speculate up to seventy, led by James), and the five Hellenistic Jewish leaders who remained from the original Seven of Acts 6 caring for their own people.[12] In contrast, the church in Antioch had five leaders of varying backgrounds, all serving with great faith and simple obedience—a catalyst for great things.

An example of how a small, agile team can quickly make decisions was how they responded as a church when they heard the prophetic news of an impending famine in Jerusalem. Without delay, they collected an offering for Barnabas and Paul to take to the saints there. Enough time had passed that the church in Antioch must have felt that Paul would be safe going to Jerusalem, especially carrying a gift for famine relief. That would be true this time, but the next time he came back to Jerusalem with gifts for relief, he was attacked by a mob. But we are getting ahead of ourselves.

The timing of this first journey back to Jerusalem was critical for the new movement. The first of the twelve original apostles—James, the son of Zebedee—by Herod's order had been martyred, "put to death with a sword." Peter was also arrested and, if not for a dramatic rescue by an angel, he too would have been killed. Not long after that, King Herod, who had sanctioned these attacks and accepted worship as if he himself were a deity, was struck down and died. Once again, a period of peaceful expansion was granted to the church in Jerusalem.

It is possible that during this stay in Jerusalem Paul had private counsel with Peter, James, and John about the revelation he had received and his calling to go to the Gentiles.[13] It is possible that the revelation he received was the one he talks about cryptically in 2 Corinthians 12, but it seems that it also had something to do with preaching the gospel to the Gentiles without their need to first become Jews. The leaders of the new church gave Barnabas and Paul the right hand of fellowship and sent them on their way to begin their mission to the Gentiles, just as Peter had been commissioned to reach the Jews.

Having completed their mission, Barnabas and Paul returned to Antioch. This time Paul had no qualms about leaving Jerusalem and may have been anxious to return to the vibrant Antioch church, composed of both Gentiles and Jews. Even though they left the financial gift behind, Paul and Barnabas did not come back empty-handed. They brought John Mark with them.

Contributing to the Team

Once he was back in the church at Antioch, Paul was one of five prophets and teachers mentioned in Acts 13: Barnabas, Simeon called Niger, Lucius of Cyrene, Manaen, and Paul. Barnabas, a Jew from Cyprus, was an encourager or exhorter and probably a prophet. This is likely why he is mentioned first, matching the word order of "*prophets* and teachers." Simeon, who was called Niger, is mentioned next. Simeon is a Jewish name, but *Niger* is Latin and means "black." He may have had African heritage and darker skin. Lucius of Cyrene is also a Latin name, and it's possible that he is the Lucius with Paul mentioned in Romans 16:21. Manaen was an elderly statesman whose name was a Greek form of the Hebrew *Menahem*, which means "comforter." He grew up with Herod the Tetrarch (Herod Antipas) who famously executed John the Baptist and met with Jesus to mock Him during His trial. Last, but certainly not least, Paul is mentioned. Mentioning Paul last may be Luke's way of telling us that Paul was a teacher while serving in Antioch, aligning his name with the word order of "prophets and *teachers*." Later Paul would describe his own gifts and calling to include being a teacher (1 Timothy 2:7; 2 Timothy 1:11).

This unique team of leaders with varied cultural backgrounds was brought together at a special time and place to change the world. Our churches and ministries today can all learn valuable lessons from this team. I believe these men played a crucial role in the expansion of God's Kingdom for these reasons:

1. They represented much more varied cultural expressions than their Jerusalem counterparts.[14] Cypriot, African, Syrian, Latin, and Israeli cultures and worldviews were all represented in this small band.

2. They were a small band with far more intimate relational connections. Small enough, however, that even with such diverse points of view they could find consensus. If they did not, having an odd number of team members meant they would always have a tie-breaker, but given their close relational connection with one another and the Holy Spirit, this was likely only needed in the worst-case scenario.

3. I believe these men had the equipping gifts mentioned in Ephesians 4:11. Mentioned by Luke are prophets and teachers—and soon some would be sent as apostles. All five gifts would likely have been at work in their ministry as the leaders pursued the fullness of Christ in active service.[15]

4. They intentionally fasted and prayed together to listen to the Lord and to serve Him. Imagine how different things would be if our church leaders today set aside agendas and simply did the same. I have often taught that if you bring the right people to the meeting, you don't need an agenda. If you find you do need an agenda to cover the important subjects, then perhaps you don't have the right people with you. The right people, all surrendered to the Spirit of Christ, will cover anything that is truly important and not allow lesser things to occupy time and talk.

5. They began with an openness to reach all people, not just Jews, and God honored that faith. In Galatians, Paul seems to indicate that Jew and Gentiles usually shared meals together. While Peter had initially broken down the barrier between Jew and Gentile, no previous church had exhibited this kind of bold interaction. The members of this church shook up the order of the world they knew, and they showed that they were more committed to following the Lord than to following their own Jewish tradition. They were not bound by their cultural walls but were free to think outside the box and love all people. The theological and cultural prejudice that the Jerusalem church displayed was not found on this team—that is,

until some of the Jerusalem leaders showed up later and infected them with legalistic doubts (Galatians 2:11–21).

With this team of prophets and teachers, Paul once again heard the voice of the Lord calling him to his mission. While they were serving the Lord, fasting, and praying, they all heard the Holy Spirit say, "Set apart for Me Barnabas and Saul for the work to which I have called them." Try to imagine how this moment felt to Paul. It was like the coach turned to him and said, "Okay, now is your moment. You are ready—go!"

Over the years I have found that some contexts are especially conducive for hearing the voice of the Lord. A small band of leaders such as this one (five is the ideal number) can be something truly special.[16]

This group and the church at Antioch became a home base for Paul for much of his adult life. It was from this place that a new and unprecedented work was about to be launched.

Your Story: Lessons of Inner Life Development

As we consider Paul's life up to this point, we see many foundational principles that apply to our spiritual development. During this stage of character formation, the people that God is conforming to His image are usually anxious to be useful. Instead, this phase is often filled with waiting, isolation, and even frustration and a sense of abandonment. In the moment this may feel wrong, but in fact, it is quite normal and right. It's an intensely formative time where listening to the Lord, abiding in Christ, and obedience are built into the disciple in a very practical manner. Future accomplishments are built on these very lessons, so they are absolutely necessary. The Lord may seem less interested in the disciples' achievements during this time because He is preparing them for future work.

The main thrust of this phase is to know God in a more personal and dynamic way. From the moment human beings first rebelled in the garden of Eden, God has been pursuing us—and in this stage, we come to recognize this. A dramatic surrender often occurs, whether that is a first-time conversion, a step into greater devotion and life service, or both. For followers of Jesus who continue to journey through increasing significance to a strong finish, this stage is characterized by recognizing and surrendering to God's overtures into their lives. Learning to listen to, hear, and obey the voice of the Lord is the most essential lesson and is foundational for all journeys to follow. All subsequent activity flows from that intimate relationship with God, not just from ambition or duty. These lessons all share one element—how the Lord gets our attention so that we can follow His leading.

Learning to Love God's Voice

Many of us, like Paul, have grown up in a religious system that encourages people to take God's word and obey it without hearing the actual voice that speaks it. This may seem like a small distinction, but it is the difference between heaven and hell. Tragically, many give their entire lives to studying the Scriptures and never hear the still small voice of God carrying the words. Paul was on that very track until he was detoured on the road to Damascus. It is possible to love the Scriptures, but not love the voice of God. What is not possible is to love the voice of God and disregard the Scriptures. When you love God's voice, you will grow in your love of the Scriptures because you will find what you love in every word.

The heart of this stage of inner life development is learning to walk closely with God, hearing and depending on God's leading rather than simply living in conformity to the principles found in His book. The Bible enlightens and sanctifies us, but it is possible to see it mainly as a textbook and the source of commands or merely a code of conduct to obey rather than as a living and active voice. Prior to knowing Jesus, Paul knew how to read, interpret, and apply the Scriptures—in fact, he was a pro at it. But this type of literary competence can result in lifeless behavior conformity instead of an inner spiritual transformation. He knew his Bible (Old Testament) but couldn't understand Jesus' voice as evidenced by the Lord's word: "It is hard for you to kick against the goads" (Acts 26:14). What Paul needed to learn experientially was how to hear God's active voice in His Word, so he could hear it constantly. Despite enormous time spent with the Scriptures, God still had to shout at Paul on the road to Damascus to be heard the first time. God is alive *now* and speaks to us in power and intimacy. We must learn to hear His voice and follow it courageously, for it will take us on the journeys He intends for our lives. Listen to Jesus and do what He says.

This is perhaps the most essential lesson for the spiritual life of a follower of Jesus. If this is hard for you, then this is what you need to devote yourself to learning now. This is not, however, a lesson learned once and applied forever. Listening to the voice of your Shepherd is merely the beginning. This is an ongoing relationship that grows in intimacy and develops over time together, so that you are constantly learning for the rest of your life. Although you will get better and better at it, the learning will continue. Just as no husband and wife should ever claim to have mastered communication to a point where there is nothing more to learn, we must continue to mature in our communication with Jesus. Get started immediately. Do not "kick against the goads" and merely use the Bible like an owner's manual to conform your actions to its directives. Find the voice of God and follow it with courage.

Radical Salvation

We are often shaped by our regrets. While all past sins are forgiven with the redemption that comes in Christ, there are some things that leave permanent marks on our lives. Wounds heal, but scars remain. In Paul's case, he would always remember Stephen's words and his death. Those scars would be redeemed for a higher purpose, but they did not just go away. Like the former addict who has a heart to reach other addicts, we may find that the things we have done and been forgiven of can play a critical role in God's plan for our future.

Paul's salvation has become a pivotal moment in history that has been examined and scrutinized by some of the greatest thinkers humanity has produced. It was such a radical change that we may be tempted to think this type of transformation is only for Paul. But we would be wrong about that.

It is important that we realize that *all* followers of Christ are *radically saved*. There is no other kind of salvation. People who were raised by Christian parents and made good moral decisions often feel salvation was less dramatic for them than for drug dealers or prostitutes who find Christ when they are at the end of their rope. This is a lie. Every salvation experience is a radical transfer of a unique soul from a kingdom of darkness into a kingdom of light, with all that entails. This profound transformation of the soul is truly the energy that propels all our spiritual formation and resulting significance. True significance does not come from better strategies or further education; it only comes from a life changed by the presence of Jesus.

If we understood and accepted God's offer of salvation when we were young, there is absolutely no reason to suffer from "testimony envy" when we hear the sensational story of the former assassin who is now preaching the love of Jesus. Our salvation is as profound as anyone else's and was purchased at the same extreme cost. God is the same powerful Redeemer to us as He is to the former satanist who now serves Christ. We have been saved from the same just and terrible penalty as much as anyone else who has been forgiven by Christ.

If our lives lack compelling testimonies of God's deliverance, it is because we are not taking enough risks for the sake of Jesus. When we step out obediently on the thin ice of risk so that God must intervene to demonstrate His love and provision for us, then we too will have great stories to tell of God's deliverance—and people will recognize that we are also radically saved by Jesus.

Mimicry

I believe Paul attempted, albeit briefly, to take over the role once filled by Stephen. This is quite common in early spiritual formation, when we are less aware of ourselves and are easily influenced by the gifts, calling, and example of others that went before us.

It was probably easy for Paul to explain all the reasons for him to take up where Stephen left off, and for a moment he attempted to do that. God had other plans for Paul and immediately sent him packing for an extended time of isolation. Emulating someone that is used by God at this stage can actually be helpful, but it should be short-lived. Just as a student-artist can learn much from copying the great masters, this is only for the purpose of training.

Don't try to be someone else. It is common for younger people to try to imitate those they admire, whether it's their character or their successful methods. This is a good thing, in many ways, as you are only learning to do things, but along the way you must become the woman or man God intends you to be and not strive to be someone else. That growth comes from consistently abiding and obeying daily and letting go of goals that are based on other people's records and abilities. I consistently remind young leaders attempting to mimic others that one of those leaders is more than enough for us all. What we truly need is the you God has in His mind, not the you that is in your own imagination at this early stage. The sooner you can let that old you die so the new one can be born, the sooner you can mature to a new phase of development.

Destiny Revelation

Some of us might receive a *destiny revelation*, as Paul did, at this stage of life. Clinton defines this as "significant acts, people, or providential circumstances or timing that hint at some future or special significance to a life and add to an awareness of a sense of destiny in a life."[17] The revelation will likely not be specific, and we will still need to be faithful in the lessons of life's journeys, just like anyone else. The destiny revelation, however, usually holds some promise of future calling that helps us get through the struggles and not be content with less.

The caution concerning destiny revelation is to let the fulfillment come to you in God's ultimate timing rather than attempting to make it happen earlier with your own determination and abilities. This is what Moses had to learn after attempting to fulfill his destiny in his own strength when, as a young man, he killed an oppressive Egyptian. He had to spend forty years in the wilderness before encountering a burning bush—then God finally began to bring his destiny to fruition. God never forgets our calling and destiny even if we do, but all the timing and means are His to decide and manifest, never ours.

Like other kinds of prophetic words, a destiny revelation always carries more weight when two or three independent witnesses can confirm it as being from the Lord. Another confirmation is when the word is delivered in a remarkable and supernatural fashion, as Paul experienced. Ananias knew who and where Paul was and what had occurred on the road, and then he proceeded to heal him of his blindness, as the Lord had ordered—this was a clear confirmation. That Paul had already received a vision of this happening is more compelling evidence that the message received was indeed from the Lord.

In the absence of such confirmation, it's wise to hold any prophetic word about our future loosely. There is one person in the universe that wants you to hear God's voice even more than you do—God. God knows how to communicate, and when He does, He wants you to understand. He will have no trouble confirming His word to you if you are open to it, but many lives have been sidelined or distracted by the absence of sound confirmation. Hearing something that you want to hear, without any confirmation, can become a hindrance that haunts you for many years to come. Hold loosely to prophetic words and wait for confirmation before you grant them weight—and especially before you order your future around them.

Foundations of Character

During this time of inner life development, growing disciples begin serving in some sort of ministry. Others notice their enthusiasm, and soon they have some type of training, either formal or informal. They learn on the job, through practice. Often, however, they do not achieve the success they desire.

In our earlier phases of spiritual development, God is not so interested in getting stuff *out* of us, like visible success. He is intent on getting stuff *into* us—our character. Character formation takes priority at this stage of development over merely learning skills or information. What we *do* is less important than who we *are*. People who use extraordinary skills, personality, and spiritual gifts to compensate for their lack of character formation are making a reservation for future collapse and loss. We are witnessing the devastation of such collapse almost daily in our churches. The character qualities Christ desires to produce in us are non-negotiable, and it is less costly to pursue them in these earlier stages. We may face the collapse of our life and ministry when we build them around our skills without having the character needed to carry such a load.

It may sound cockeyed, but sometimes we are saved from the very success we have been praying for during these early years. Achieving what we consider success can be an impediment to future growth and learning. It is far easier to transition and grow from failure than from success. If we achieve all the accomplishments we want at this early stage, we may never discover the more meaningful fruitfulness later. We might spend the rest of our lives protecting our early success or trying to relive it. Growing out of initial success to another phase of maturity often means sacrificing that success before we can move on. This is so hard that most people are unwilling to do it. For all these reasons, God doesn't answer all our prayers for success during this formative stage. He is our wise Father, full of love, who has greater plans for our lives than we do. If God answered all our prayers at this stage, the foundation for far greater success in the future would not be laid.

Because God focuses more on character formation than on ministry success, there may be early tests of our readiness for future journeys. These tests are checks of integrity, of obedience to do what God asks, and of the ability to hear and discern God's directions. If we do well with the tests, we will move forward into other journeys. If not, we will experience the same lessons again, with greater pressure. These tests are not because God doesn't already know what is in store or what is in us. These checks are to make clear to us what we are made of and what is important. When our character is challenged, we get to decide the limits of how far we, as a man or woman of God, will bend without breaking under the pressures of life. A proper response to God's teaching and testing will result in greater responsibility and opportunity. As Jesus said in the parable of the talents to those who passed the test: "Well done, good and faithful slave. You were faithful with a few things, I will put you in charge of many things; enter the joy of your master" (Matthew 25:21). It is one thing to trust God. It is an even greater thing when God can trust us, and that takes some testing and training early in our inner life development.

Isolation

Even superstars sit on the bench for a time. When we are immature or inexperienced, we have no idea what we do not know. We tend to think we can do anything, but we are ignorant about how unprepared we truly are. God, in His infinite love and wisdom, often removes all options so that we are forced to wait and learn as we receive the wisdom and experience necessary for future work. None of us would ever intentionally sign up for this, so God imposes it on us when it is most important for our development.

Isolation is a tool God uses for us to learn some of the lifelong lessons necessary for future works. We can be removed from visible service or leadership, usually for an extended time, so that we experience God in a deeper way. This can be quite frustrating and would not normally be our choice, which is why it is usually thrust upon us in a way that is not calculated or anticipated. This isolation feels like punishment, but it is not. Indeed, it is the opposite of punishment. Jesus refers to pruning His disciples like a vine, not because we aren't bearing fruit but precisely because we are. Why? So that we can ultimately bear much more fruit (John 15:2). God wants to expand our capacity for production, and this is how He does it. If we cannot *learn how to learn* at this stage, then the other journeys will be put on hold.

Isolation calls us to listen, learn, and lean on God. It is an investment in future success. It is a deepening of our relationship with God so that the rest of the journeys are marked by this necessary intimacy. During isolation God removes from us all other crutches and supports so that we find we have all we need in Jesus alone. That is one of the greatest lessons anyone can ever learn, but it can only really be learned in lonely places—when Jesus is all we have left. When we realize this truth, it is something that can never be unlearned and will serve us well for the rest of our days.

When the time is right, and the lessons of isolation are learned, God makes that known. My good friend and ministry partner Dezi Baker calls this isolation experience "the long and lonely road." Often but not always, we are brought out of isolation as suddenly and unexpectedly as we were brought into it. We do not emerge from the long, lonely road the same as we entered it. The lessons learned on this road are so deep that they become part of us, so that we don't have to think about them to put them into practice—they become who we are.

While struggling through these tough lessons, it is normal to feel frustrated and aggrieved. But after the lessons are learned, we may have warm affection for the memories of these very times.

There is little that mentors can do to alleviate the pain of this formative stage. It doesn't help when they share the lessons they learned, complete with tales of struggles in isolation and frustration. It is far more helpful for more mature people to feel our pain, listen to our stories, and be understanding of and empathetic toward our hurts. But even these comforts are sometimes not available for the disciple during this phase. Jesus, the Great Physician, prescribes the hardship of this struggle, and to take it away would be detrimental to the spiritual formation of the Christ-follower. It is called "isolation" for a reason. Isolation can only pass on its precious jewels in solitude on the long and lonely road.

The type of intimacy God desires us to have with Him can only be learned experientially. During isolation we may constantly ask for the lesson to be learned if for no other reason than to end the struggle and pain of being alone. We will be tempted to think that we can learn some facts and it will all come to an end, but that is naive. A Bible study cannot teach us what we need to learn from isolation. Even reading this or similar books will not pass on to us the lessons that can only be learned in the experience itself. The only solution is calling out to God and finding His presence to be the remedy for our loneliness. And we cannot find that solution without first being alone— and being alone long enough for our utter dependence on Him to sink deep into the marrow of our bones.

We will discover in those slow and difficult days that we are truly not alone. Though we feel forgotten by all the people we thought we were so important to, God will never leave us or forget about us. That is a lesson that cannot simply be assimilated from a sermon we've heard or a book we've read. No matter how long the trial lasts, that lesson is worth every minute in the struggle. It will be the core of who we are to become and will make us into an unshakeable force for His Kingdom. It is the only path to that kind of strength.

The good news is that for most of us this stage has an expiration date. It is a foundation for what is to come, and God intends the investment placed in us during these early phases to bear even greater fruit in the journeys to come.

Paul was about to ascend to a whole new level of significance on a global scale. The next ten years of Paul's life would turn the world upside down, but they were built on the previous ten years of isolation and seeming futility. We cannot have world impact without first experiencing the personal impact of our earlier journeys. But that is not to say that at the end of isolation, all our lessons will have been learned. Many more are to come, built on the foundations of those learned in struggle and isolation.

Radical Obedience

An essential quality for us to learn from this part of Paul's story wasn't exemplified by Paul but by his friend Barnabas. Luke says, "And he left for Tarsus to look for Saul; and when he had found him, he brought him to Antioch" (Acts 11:25-26). A willingness to travel far—a minimum of 300 miles round trip on foot—because of the Holy Spirit's leading is evidence of the kind of spirituality God can use in incredible ways. Barnabas might have been only a small footnote in the Bible if he hadn't been radically obedient at this very moment. Because he did follow the Spirit, he is a key character in the New Testament that people still read about, honor, and learn from two thousand years later.

Most of us are far too bound to our immediate circumstances to even be open to such direction from the Holy Spirit. Our busy schedules, routines, expectations, and obligations won't allow for it. We are tempted to think that such a radical response is foolish. Think about it. If Barnabas had stayed in Antioch as he had been directed—by the leadership of the Jerusalem church no less—no one would ever have questioned him, and the great work God accomplished through his partnership with Paul would have been delayed longer or even lost. We don't know for certain, but it is entirely plausible that he was severely questioned by many when he left to search for Paul. He listened to Jesus and obeyed even if no one else understood why.

The internet, mobile phones, email, and video conferencing have all been convenient and useful for the Kingdom of God. But these tools also tend to cement us in place. Certainly, it would have been easier for Barnabas to just send an email to Paul, but there is something incredibly powerful in immediate, radical obedience.

We must learn to walk in instantaneous obedience even if it takes us many miles from our original place. Such obedience to the impressions of the Spirit can be used by God in many ways. Do not underestimate radical obedience.

I believe from my own experience that this obedience can empower the angelic world to push back entrenched darkness for the cause of expanding God's Kingdom of light. Spiritual doors sealed shut for centuries may open for the gospel. When we stay in predictable patterns, the enemy may be allowed to hold sway over regions without challenge. Angelic forces are bound to us and our unmoving status quo. When we break away without warning and follow the Spirit's leading, the enemy is taken by surprise and falls back on his heels. Angels go forth with us on offense into hostile territory, and the spirit world is turned upside down. Frankly, I think the angels long for this, and our enemy is terrified by the mere thought of it.

The darkness we all experience in our world today is demanding us to be this kind of spiritually sensitive people. I believe we are entering into times when this type of immediate obedience will be essential and hopefully much more prevalent.

Listen and obey. You will not regret it. If you do not, you still may not regret it, but you will also never know what could have been. You may miss out on some of your greatest moments and eventually die without even knowing what could have happened.

I challenge you to try in simple ways to build up your sensitivity to the Holy Spirit's direction. This will lead to a level of obedience that God will use in miraculous and dramatic fashion. Try going for a drive without any destination and turn down any and all streets where His voice directs. See where He takes you. Learn to become instantly obedient to the Spirit's lead. This makes you the kind of agent God can use for great works in His Kingdom.

Foundation Laid, Ready for Launch

As we get ready to look at Paul's first intentional trip to spread the gospel, take a moment to reflect on all Jesus had already done in the apostle's life to prepare him. Now use the reflection questions on the following page to evaluate God's past and current work in your own life. Praise Him for His faithfulness in developing your character so far and anticipate what Kingdom impact He is equipping you to accomplish. Let's dive in and trace Paul's adventures on this initial journey.

 **New Life and Early Ministry Reflections**
Here are some reflection questions to ask yourself:

- Can you describe the radical change in your life as a result of choosing to embrace Christ? What previous qualities are diminishing, and what emerging qualities are replacing them? What is there in your life that can only be ascribed to the presence of God?
- How has God revealed His calling on your life? Can you articulate what He is telling you in a passionate and convincing manner?
- Can you identify people you once tried to emulate? How are you honoring their example while developing your own style?
- Have you found it easier and fulfilling to work within the framework of a diverse team? Have you felt the synergy that comes when different gifts and minds come together for a mission greater than each of you independently? If not, ask God to give you this special blessing, and remain open to it.
- Have you experienced some isolation where God and God alone is speaking into your life? Can you explain some previous opinions you held and how those have been replaced with completely new ideas from God?
- Can you identify a moment when you radically obeyed the prompting of God's Spirit? What happened as a result? If not, can you commit yourself to do so very soon?

CHAPTER 3

THE FIRST JOURNEY

For This I Was Born

> *It's what you learn after you know it all that really counts.*
> —John Wooden

> *Paul, an apostle (not sent from men nor through the agency of man, but through Jesus Christ and God the Father, who raised Him from the dead).*
> —Paul to the churches started on his first journey
>   (Galatians 1:1)

A few years ago, I found myself on a missionary journey—not from Antioch but to that ancient city. The Lord had impressed several leaders to visit Syrian Antioch to seek God together; we wanted to hear from Him about the way missions are done in the world today. Our modest hotel was between the ruins that once were the docks of Seleucia to the east and the Mediterranean Sea to the west. The hotel's location would have been submerged when Barnabas and Saul set sail on their important mission. Two thousand years of runoff from the nearby mountains have pushed the sea's edge several hundred yards from the ancient docks, which now are simply a wall in a field where pumpkins are grown.

I gazed across the field at those large, timeworn stones and tried to visualize what Paul, Barnabas, and Barnabas's cousin John Mark (Colossians 4:10) must have looked like as they waited there to board the ship that would take them on a new journey. In my imagination, I pictured Barnabas sitting and looking confident—he was headed to his homeland.

I pictured his cousin seated beside him, less confident, unable to take his eyes off Paul who was pacing back and forth like a caged lion with his gaze on the horizon. How would it have felt to be about to embark on a trip without any idea of what to expect? No one had ever done what they were about to attempt.

As far as we know, this was the first time a local church, led by the Holy Spirit, had sent a missionary team for the purpose of making disciples of people overseas—an expedition that would result in the starting of indigenous churches, which in turn would start others. Paul had often traveled before, but this was his first missionary journey. All his previous journeys—trips to Jerusalem as a child, travels to Damascus under orders as a persecutor, his return to Tarsus, his trip to Jerusalem from Antioch bringing a gift for famine relief—were trainings for this day, his first true missionary journey. Fifteen years after Paul's encounter with the Lord on the road to Damascus, God Himself finally said, "Go, now. This is what I have called you to. You're ready." The rest of history would refer to this as Paul's first missionary journey, but it was the first of its kind for anyone.

Paul's Story: The First Journey

Around the spring of AD 47, Barnabas and Paul, along with John Mark, went to Seleucia and took a ship from there to Cyprus. They landed in Salamis and began preaching in the synagogues. John Mark was their helper, but I assume that this didn't mean he carried their luggage. I imagine that he was to be an actual eyewitness of the things preached about Jesus and perhaps a functioning scribe keeping a diary of all that was occurring on this adventure. These notes could have been of great help to Luke later as he pieced together these events from interviews, testimonies, and perhaps even Mark's short journal entries. Eventually this young man would author the Gospel of Mark, so he had some writing skills.

Although Barnabas was from Cyprus, he soon started to take a back seat to Paul's leadership. That may have been because of a problem which was true even of Jesus—a prophet is not welcome in his hometown (Luke 4:24). It may also have been because Paul had stepped into a groove that all could recognize, and Barnabas was both smart and humble enough to ride the momentum. Given Barnabas's reputation in Scripture, I favor the latter explanation. He truly lived to encourage and empower others in discovering their own purpose in God's redemptive mission.

When Paul and the team had gone from east to west through the island, they arrived at Paphos, a city that was the capital of the island. There they came across a magician, a Jewish false prophet whose name was Bar-Jesus, which literally means "Son of Jesus." This man was an advisor of sorts to the Roman proconsul, Sergius Paulus, who was a very intelligent man. In his Pauline biography, John Pollock explains that Sergius Paulus had a scientific mind, which Pliny the Elder cited as an authority in his *Natural History*.[1] Sergius Paulus was curious and wanted to hear more from the apostles, so he requested that they come and share their message with him.

In the counsel of the proconsul, however, was Bar-Jesus. Clearly, the missionaries objected to this false prophet being named "Son of Jesus" or "Son of a Savior." In Acts 13, Luke calls him Elymas—perhaps a Semitic word for sorcerer, or possibly even his given name—rather than Bar-Jesus. Paul goes further and twists it around and calls him "son of the devil."

In any case, the sorcerer tried to dissuade the proconsul from hearing Paul's message, probably because he was afraid of losing influence over such an important politician. Paul, full of the Holy Spirit, turned his attention to the disruptive influence and proclaimed, "You who are full of all deceit and fraud, you son of the devil, you enemy of all righteousness, will you not cease to make crooked the straight ways of the Lord?" From Paul's charge, it seems clear that the sorcerer was attempting to counter what the apostles were telling Sergius Paulus.

Paul was not done with him. He went on to say, "Now, behold, the hand of the Lord is upon you, and you will be blind and not see the sun for a time." With that, a mist and a darkness fell on the false prophet, essentially blinding him. It is appropriate that one so spiritually blind would suffer physical blindness as a judgment.

It is possible that Elymas found spiritual enlightenment because of his physical blindness. The blindness was not a sudden blackness but is described as first a mist that came over him followed by darkness. Only Elymas himself could really know what his own eyes were seeing or not seeing. There is a good chance that he later turned to follow Jesus as a result and gave Luke his own recollection of the account. Of course, this is conjecture, but not without some basis. In Luke's account, Paul does seem furious at the man, but we must remember Paul's experience of having gone blind by the hand of God and finding new enlightenment as a result. Personally, I can't help thinking that Paul was empathetic to a religious persecutor who wanted to disrupt the Lord's work. He surely would not have forgotten his own experience of temporary blindness (Acts 9:9).

Whatever happened with Elymas, one thing is certain—a door opened for the gospel in the proconsul's court. Sergius Paulus, hearing the message and seeing the powerful miracle of judgment against Elymas, believed in Christ. This was a divine appointment that granted important access for the missionaries and also revealed something about themselves.

Beginning at this point, Saul was called Paul (his Roman name). It may simply be coincidence that Paul chose his Roman name over his Jewish name after meeting such a powerful leader who bore the same name. Perhaps he thought that his Roman name would be better received in a Gentile world. For whatever reason, from this point on he was known as Paul and apparently took the lead in the missionary work, with Barnabas taking a more supportive role. The mission began with the Holy Spirit saying, "Set apart for Me Barnabas and Saul." Now Luke refers to them here as "Paul and his companions" (Acts 13:13). Paul suddenly blossomed, as if he had been born for this work—which, of course, he had been (Galatians 1:15). Most spiritual gifts are only truly discovered when we launch out into the world and try them out to see how they fit. This role as an apostolic missionary fit Paul perfectly. Everyone could see it.

After the experience in Paphos, the team apparently went directly to the Galatian region of Asia Minor. The New Testament scholar Eckhard Schnabel suggests that Sergius Paulus may have given them important contacts in Antioch of Pisidia.[2] This may well be the case, since they seemed set on this course and did not stop or detour in spite of the long journey up a steep mountain even though it's possible Paul was afflicted by a physical illness (Galatians 4:13–14). Once there, they began preaching the gospel in the synagogues again.

When Jesus instructed the disciples in how to bring the gospel of His

Kingdom to new people, He told them that they were to look for "a man of peace." If such a person were found, the missionary was to stay and focus on reaching all those relationally connected to him (Luke 10:1–16). The gospel in the New Testament often spread through a web of relational connections called an *oikos*, a word that our Bibles translate as "household," even though it can have other meanings beyond a single family. It was often used to refer to a sort of network of close relational connections that would include a person's slaves, intimate friends, work associates, and relatives.[3] All of Jesus' teaching on spreading the gospel of His Kingdom follows the tracks laid down from *oikos* to *oikos*.

This particular teaching of Jesus is expounded most fully in Luke 10.[4] It's logical that Luke would illustrate it in real practice in Acts. Luke has already demonstrated this powerful method in earlier chapters and will do so again in later ones. Some strategic basics will never change in service of Christ, and this relational approach is one of them. Jesus' teaching about reaching *oikos* after *oikos* through the person of peace is universal and still as relevant as ever.

In the second volume of his *Early Christian Mission*, Schnabel establishes that there was a familial connection between Sergius Paulus and Sergii Paulii, who both owned estates in the region of Vetissus, which was in the province of Galatia in central Anatolia.[5] It is entirely likely that after Sergius Paulus found salvation by faith in Jesus, he wanted others in his family to also hear this message of hope; this desire may have set a path for the missionaries and opened some relational doors for the gospel in this new territory. If true, it would explain the sudden directness with which the apostolic band headed up the steep incline to Antioch of Pisidia.

From Paphos, the missionary band set sail for what is now called the Gulf of Antalya and then seven miles up the Cestrus River to Perga. Perga was a great city whose ruins are still impressive. At this point, John Mark chose to abandon the mission and return home. Luke does not say why.

On to Galatia

Paul and Barnabas went on the long climb to Antioch of Pisidia, 3,600 feet above sea level. On the first Sabbath after their arrival, Paul and

Barnabas entered the synagogue and took their seats. As was customary, visitors were invited to speak. Because Paul was a former Pharisee who had been mentored by Gamaliel, I imagine that the members of the synagogue might have been anxious to hear from him. And he certainly did not disappoint—not that day anyway. Paul greeted the people in customary fashion, but, against the tradition of the synagogues of the day, he also recognized the God-fearers in the crowd. In Acts 14 Luke records Paul's message in detail, showing by the emphasis on Israel's history that Paul spoke to a primarily Jewish audience. Paul's speech also mirrored Stephen's address in Acts 7 in many ways. It was as if Paul desired to continue the impact of the life he was partly responsible for cutting short. The memory of Stephen would follow Paul all his days, but it would be used in positive and powerful ways.

All who heard the message seemed to be pleased. In fact, many people surrounded Paul afterward, wanting to hear more and practically begging him to return the following week. When he went to the synagogue the next Sabbath, Luke says, "nearly the whole city assembled to hear the word of the Lord." But this infuriated the regular synagogue members who were consumed with jealousy and so contradicted Paul. In response, Paul and Barnabas announced boldly: "It was necessary that the word of God be spoken to you first; since you repudiate it and judge yourselves unworthy of eternal life, behold, we are turning to the Gentiles" (Acts 14:46).

Paul and Barnabas then left the synagogue and probably preached the message to a large crowd of receptive Gentiles and Jews, many of whom believed. In the very next verse Luke tells us, "And the word of the Lord was being spread through the whole region." The reign of Christ spread in every direction. Perhaps part of this initial success was due to Paul and Barnabas following up on the contacts given to them by Sergius Paulus. Soon, though, the Jewish leaders instigated a persecution against Paul and Barnabas and drove them out of that region.

We see this pattern repeated during the rest of Paul's journeys. He would proclaim the message in a synagogue if one could be found. In a short time, the Jews would reject this new message, but a few would join Paul as he began sharing his message with the Gentiles, where he would see his greatest effectiveness. The Jews who rejected him would not leave him alone, though, but would stir up controversy around him until finally persecution and beatings would chase him on to the next city. Antioch of Pisidia was the first city where this sequence took place.

As Paul and Barnabas were chased out of Antioch, they obeyed the Lord by shaking the dust off their feet in protest (Luke 10:11) as they started off to the next town—Iconium. They stayed there sharing Jesus to such an extent that the whole city seemed divided over their message. Some of the people threatened to mistreat them and stone them, and so they left. The pattern was repeated in the regions of Lycaonia, Lystra, and Derbe. Luke records some details of what occurred in those places in Acts 14.[6]

From Stardom to Stoning

While preaching in Lystra, Paul recognized that a man who had been lame his whole life had enough faith to be saved and healed. He stopped his message, gazed down at the man, and commanded him to rise and walk. The man jumped to his feet, healed.

The crowd was amazed at this miracle—so amazed that people in the crowd began speaking excitedly in the Lycaonian language, which Paul and Barnabas did not understand. As it turned out, the people thought that Paul and Barnabas were the fulfillment of a local legend concerning the god Zeus and his son and spokesman, Hermes. According to the story, those Greek gods had come to the area in the form of mortal men, and the only ones who showed them hospitality had been a couple named Philemon and Baucis. The gods punished all except this couple. The Lycaonians, familiar with the story, saw this miracle and assumed that Barnabas was Zeus, and that Paul was Hermes because he was talking so much more, which they expected from the messenger god Hermes. The crowd did not want to repeat the mistake of not recognizing the gods, so the local priest of Zeus, whose temple was just outside the city, brought oxen and garlands to the gates to offer sacrifices to honor Paul and Barnabas.

Once the apostles figured out what was going on, they tore their clothes, which was a traditional Jewish cultural expression of dismay when someone heard blasphemy. They ran out into the crowd to persuade the people that they were just men, like all of them. It took some doing, but they managed to quiet the crowd just as some Jews from the previous town arrived, spotted the two, and convinced the crowd that Paul and Barnabas were not gods but charlatans.

In no time, Paul and Barnabas went from "gods" to "goads" and provoked a sharp reaction from the crowd, which turned quickly into a mob and then a gang of murderers. Some people spontaneously picked up stones and began throwing them at Paul. They continued stoning Paul until he collapsed. The crowd grabbed his apparently lifeless body and dragged it out past the city boundary. Those who had believed, along with Barnabas, gathered around Paul's body; perhaps Lois, Eunice, and a young man named Timothy were in this group, since they were from this area (2 Timothy 3:10–11).

Many people wonder if Paul, who was left for dead, actually died from the attack and was resurrected. Some believe that this was the occasion when he went up to the third heaven, as recounted in 2 Corinthians 12. The timing is not right, however, for that experience is said to have happened fourteen years before Paul wrote that epistle, which would put it around AD 42, during Paul's dark days in Tarsus. Luke is careful not to say that Paul died during this event, and so perhaps we should join Luke in his caution. Had this been a legal execution, the authorities would have verified his death; as it was, the attackers seemed in a hurry to leave the scene of the crime.

In any event, the small group that gathered around Paul was surprised to see him rise, brush off what was left of the rocks and dust, and walk back into town. Luke does not record that anyone said anything at this astonishing turn of events. He just goes on to tell us that the next day Paul and Barnabas left and journeyed thirty miles to Derbe.

Near the end of his life, Paul reminded Timothy of the beatings he had witnessed Paul receiving in Antioch (of Pisidia), Iconium, and Lystra (2 Timothy 3:10–11). It appears that Timothy was traveling with the missionaries during these times. While speculative, a possible explanation is that the incident with the confusion over the local tongue prompted the apostles to take Timothy along with them so that they had a "local" to help with the language and culture. Being from a culturally mixed home (his father was Gentile and his mother Jewish), Timothy probably could speak more than one language and could also adapt well in cross-cultural settings. If so, this would have been the young lad's trial journey, with the thought that if he fared well, they might call upon him in the future for even more work. Translators learn on a deeper level than their audience because they hear the words, consider what the words mean, and then find appropriate ways to express the same thought in the other language. From this moment, Timothy was launched into a life-long apprenticeship. Little did they all know how faithful this boy would come to be, and how Paul would adopt him as his own son (1 Cor. 4:17; 1 Timothy 1:18; 2 Timothy 1:2, 2:1). In fact, if this assumption is true, Timothy would be the only person to accompany Paul on all of his missionary journeys.

At some point close to this time, Paul became ill, perhaps as a result of the stoning because it doesn't appear to be an infectious illness. Writing to the churches of Galatia, he says, "But you know that it was because of a bodily illness that I preached the gospel to you the first time; and that which was a trial to you in my bodily condition you did not despise or loathe, but you received me as an angel of God, as Christ Jesus Himself." Whatever the problem was, it affected his eyes. He goes on to say, "For I bear you witness that, if possible, you would have plucked out your eyes and given them to me" (Galatians 4:13–15). But still he preached the good news. He would later say to these people, "I bear on my body the brand-marks of Jesus" (Galatians 6:17).

The Long Way Home

Derbe was the furthest point of this journey. After making some disciples there, Paul and Barnabas decided it was time to return home. From Derbe, it would not have been far to travel overland across the mountains to Tarsus and then around the bay to Antioch. Their intention, however, was to return not merely to Antioch but to all the new churches started on this trip.

The apostles were feeling the burden of the lack of leadership in these new churches, and so they went back to strengthen each one in any way they could, even though they faced the threat of further persecution. Luke says that they appointed elders in each church from among the new converts.

From Antioch of Pisidia the team ventured back down the pass into Pamphilia. This time they stopped in Perga to share their message of Jesus. They then made their way to the harbor in the city that is today called Antalya in Turkey and found a boat to Antioch.

When Paul and Barnabas eventually arrived back at their home church in Antioch, they celebrated by telling everyone about the wonders of their journey. Luke says that they spent a long time with the disciples there. It was during this time that Peter likely made a visit described in Galatians. He freely sat at the table with the Gentiles and enjoyed fellowship—that is, until some judgmental religious leaders arrived from the Jerusalem church. These men, who claimed to have been sent by James, insisted that everyone who believed the gospel, including the Gentile converts, should follow the Mosaic Law. Their presence set the leaders in Antioch on edge. Most likely, in an attempt to keep peace among the brethren (and out of respect for James, the Lord's brother), Peter and some of the other Jewish leaders stopped dining with the Gentile believers. Paul points out that even Barnabas removed himself from the Gentile table. There is nothing like a religious judgmental spirit to dampen joy and ruin authentic relationships.

This infuriated Paul. Maybe some of the believers simply thought of this compromise as a way to keep the peace, but Paul saw it as a direct attack on the gospel for which he had suffered and would ultimately die. In a public setting, he challenged Peter directly. He called him on his hypocrisy by asking him a straightforward question: "If you, being a Jew, live like the Gentiles and not like the Jews, how is it that you compel the Gentiles to live like Jews?" Peter must have responded well to Paul's rebuke, however, because within a short time he would openly support Paul and his work in the Jerusalem church as they wrestled against legalism.

This incident brought this important issue to a head. To solve the matter of what place Jewish law would play in the life of the new Gentile Christians, the Antioch church sent Paul and Barnabas to Jerusalem for meetings with the leaders there. Even before they left for Jerusalem, Paul received word that the new churches in Galatia had fallen under deceptive teaching from religious legalists who questioned Paul's authority as an apostle and his gospel of grace. Before going to Jerusalem, Paul wrote a scathing letter to the new Christians in Galatia, rebuking them for abandoning the gospel in favor of the law.[7] It was becoming apparent to Paul, however, that it was problematic to make disciples and move on without first establishing on-site leadership to initially guide them in learning important basic precepts and practices. As we will see in the following chapter, on his next journey he would attempt a new strategy that was meant to avoid this problem.

When Paul and Barnabas went to this council in Jerusalem, they told the elders their story of the great wonders that God had done to verify the gospel for these Gentiles. Peter was quick to add that he supported this new work, and he recounted his own example of how God had chosen him to bring the gospel to the Gentiles. Finally, James spoke up, quoting Old Testament evidence and suggesting a solution that seemed to satisfy everyone.

The council meetings in Jerusalem were about more than the question of ritual practices. They were about even more than deciding whether Christianity would remain simply a sect of Judaism by making all the Gentile Christians become Jews. These meetings were truly about whether our souls are sanctified by God's grace or by our own works, and that is the single greatest battle of the New Testament. This was no less than a war over the gospel itself. Fortunately for all of us, the wisdom of these leaders and the Holy Spirit prevailed (Acts 15:28), with a decision that did not fracture the church or undermine the gospel. In the end, it was settled that Gentile sanctification did not require the keeping of the Mosaic Law, which had been given to Israel. This allowed for two separate Christian lifestyles, Jewish and non-Jewish, something that would provide personal tension but also freedom to Paul in his ministry for the rest of his days.

Nevertheless, James's pronouncement and later teachings did not truly satisfy the judgmental Jewish Christians' point of view, and Paul would never be relieved of their constant hounding. But now Paul had a document directly from Peter, James the Elder, and the Jerusalem church, verifying that the Gentiles did not need to become Jews in order to be Christians. Paul and Barnabas returned home, rejoicing in the good news.

Your Story: Lessons of the First Journey

Paul and Barnabas's first journey was not only a first venture into cross-cultural overseas missionary activity on behalf of the church but also a great example of a new leader's first officially sanctioned ministry. If we look carefully through the correct lenses, we may all see a bit of ourselves in this expedition. In this section I will use the description of a "first-journey person," or a "first-journey leader" to describe the common lessons learned during this stage of spiritual formation.

The First Track Is Often the Fast Track

Paul and Barnabas covered close to 1,500 miles in one year. The first-journey person tends to be in a hurry. Like a shaken bottle of soda opened, the release of the pressure built up in preparation for the mission tends to explode in a flurry of activity. For the person who is growing as a disciple and beginning to lead, it is an opportunity to try out all the things he or she only dreamed of in the days waiting for this moment. It is quite common for a first-journey leader to see the first assignment as a stepping-stone to later roles.

Lots of Activity

The first-journey servant's appetite for ministry is insatiable. Every opportunity to serve is swallowed whole. The high level of passion during the first journey often produces a lot of exertion and motion and even some fruitfulness. Raw enthusiasm and pure adrenalin, even undisciplined and without focus, can still accomplish much. Many churches were launched during Paul's first trip. It is often the case that God works in spite of the first-journey person, who may substitute lots of ministry activity for true intimacy with God.

First-journey people often go after spiritual opportunity rather than letting it come to them. They expend more energy in shorter bursts, with less fruit to show for their efforts in the end. This is why some of the fruit that comes at this stage of maturity appears to come about as if by accident rather than as the result of an intentional strategy. I am convinced that God often saves us from our own ambitions during this phase because at these earlier stages of growth we do not have the perspective to really understand what success is, and our spiritual strength is not developed enough to carry it even if we did. Of course, there is fruit and success on the first journey, but it is small compared to what is to come.

This is not to take anything away from Paul and Barnabas's journey, but the exciting church-planting work of this trip resulted in weak and struggling churches. And Luke does not even mention Timothy in his account of this journey, even though we know Paul visited Derbe, Timothy's hometown. It is hard to imagine Timothy's name coming up when Barnabas and Paul delivered the reports of their adventures to the churches in Antioch and Jerusalem. Not until the second journey did Paul realize the potential of this young man, but it was during even later journeys that this fruit came to be of monumental significance. Timothy would wind up being a lasting and powerful gift to the Kingdom of God, and his relationship with Paul is fruit from this first journey.

Weaker Disciples and Churches

Because first-journey people often do the work all by themselves, the people they influence may develop an unhealthy dependence upon the leader. This dependence can stunt the growth of the new disciples.

The churches that were begun on Paul's first journey to the Galatian region obviously didn't have strong leadership, partly because the apostles won converts and then left shortly thereafter. That's why Paul and Barnabas felt the need to go back and visit them again expressly to appoint leaders (Acts 14:23). Then they felt the need to visit them yet again (during the second journey) to strengthen them (Acts 15:36), even after Paul's stern letter (the Galatians epistle) and the letter from the Jerusalem council (Acts 16:1–6). These people were visited a fourth time on Paul's third journey (Acts 18:23). In case you weren't keeping score, that's three return visits after the initial church plant plus two strong letters over the course of a few years. These spiritual families of new disciples were not as self-sufficient as those that Paul began on later journeys. In fact, as I will attempt to demonstrate, Paul recognized the shortcomings of this first-journey strategy and made adjustments in later missions to compensate.

First-journey disciples are drawn to do good work and want to do it well. This experience provides good learning for them but doesn't empower others or reproduce fruitfulness because they do all the work themselves. Their new disciples are trained to receive ministry but not to reproduce it. The result is weaker disciples that need special help from the outside to fill a leadership vacuum, leaving them vulnerable to strong voices that are less trustworthy, such as occurred with these first churches in Galatia (Galatians 1:7-9; 3:1).

Identity Crisis

It is natural at this stage of development for the young-in-the-faith Christ-follower to look at more mature leaders with admiration and even a desire to emulate their success in ministry. Mimicry was something we saw in the earlier phase, but some of these habits linger and raise their heads in later phases as well.

First-journey leaders do not yet have the experience and maturity to realize fully who they are as a person or a leader. They are only beginning to form their own style and reputation, so they often latch on to the successful work of others who are further along.

First-journey people tend to believe that the results they are hoping for will depend on what they do, and so they often engage in active imitation of the successful work of others. First-journeyers are often looking for practical "how to's" at seminars and conferences. Any helpful practice or strategy that they can immediately employ to gain a step up is desirable. Eventually, if they progress in their development, they come to see some of the flaws of this approach.

There were few examples available for Paul and Barnabas to observe and imitate. They were pioneers and had little to draw on and methodically follow. The words of Stephen still rang in Paul's ears at this time, I believe. He was yearning to emulate Stephen as was evident in the striking similarity of his sermon and Stephen's. Luke only records one sermon Paul delivered on this first journey, but he gave plenty of others earlier in the trip. While it is speculative, it is quite possible that Paul often copied Stephen's style of preaching in this first journey to both honor his predecessor but also to start to build his own effective voice. Obviously, Stephen still held a deep place in Paul's heart.

All musicians begin by playing and singing the songs that others have written before them. Eventually, some gain the skill to write their own music and gain their own voice and style. Doing covers of the songs of admired heroes can be valuable, but the best musicians are not satisfied with copying the songs of others. This is only a start.

The most important lessons of our lives do not come from books, seminars, or our mimicry of others but from our own hard-won lessons of failure, frustration, and fighting on. In later journeys we see that Paul's own voice comes out in his preaching, and his style grows far beyond his original inspiration. It is only here in this first journey that we see such similarity.

Emerging Influence

Don't try to be someone you are not; become comfortable in your own skin. Even though first-journey people are not anywhere near the pinnacle of maturity in their work, they are still leaders who are serving the Lord, and they do produce results. People notice their gifts and their passion, and first-journey people will influence others, just not as much or as significantly as they will on later journeys.

It is interesting to watch how Paul emerged as the true leader on this first trip. The journey began with the Holy Spirit saying, "Set apart for Me Barnabas and Saul for the work I have called them to." The team that left was referred to as Barnabas and Saul (Acts 13:7), but as the journey progressed the terminology transposed to "Paul and Barnabas" (Acts 13:42, 43, 46). At one point the team was referred to as "Paul and his companions" (Acts 13:13), and Barnabas became just a companion to Paul in his work.

Barnabas was a bit further down the developmental path than Paul. We simply must admire his humility, as demonstrated by his encouraging Paul to lead. The "Son of Encouragement," as he was called, was always looking to make others around him blossom, and with Paul he succeeded. Apparently, he also succeeded with John Mark since Paul would later comment repeatedly on John Mark's effectiveness in spite of refusing his service on the second trip (Colossians 4:10; Philemon 24; 2 Timothy 4:11).

First Journey Reflections

Here are some reflection questions for those who have been on the first journey:

- Have you found yourself in a hurry to serve God as if you need to tick off each box before you can move on? Have tasks driven your development so far?
- Do you find yourself working on a wide scale with a great diversity of challenges?
- In your work, do you find that other people notice how good you are at the job? Do they comment about it and prefer that you continue doing it?
- Is delegation hard for you? Do you find it difficult to trust others to do the work to your standards? Do you think that you can do the job better and faster than others so you just plow through without concern for the development of the people around you?
- Are the results of your work more important to you than the process of doing it?

The first journey is probably the least effective journey of our life, but it is necessary. On the first journey, we gain the practical know-how that later will be passed on to others. For this reason, none of us can skip the trip. It will bear fruit that lasts, we hope, but we also hope that it will not be the most productive period of our life.

Each of life's journeys has its own progression. The man who embarked from the harbor in Seleucia was not the same when he returned a year later—even his name was changed. We may not experience that level of transformation, but like Paul, we will discover that the lessons we learn on our first journey will bear significant consequences for our second.

CHAPTER 4

THE SECOND JOURNEY

Learning Can Be a Pain

> *If you want to make God laugh, tell him your plans.*
> —Woody Allen

> *For to me, to live is Christ and to die is gain.*
> —The apostle Paul (Philippians 1:21)

Paul's first journey, with all its hardships, was marked by so much apparent success that it is hard to imagine Paul trying to fix any part of his strategy. So many new disciples and churches, so many miracles and breakthroughs—surely he would do everything the same on his second trip, right?

Success can be seductive. Contrary to expectations, great accomplishments do not always leave us feeling secure but often quite the opposite—strangely insecure. We may be prone to think our achievements were a happy accident. We may feel that our success was undeserved and if people really knew who we were they would not respond well to us. We may feel like all that was gained could just as easily be lost. Because of these and other reasons, most people set out to repeat the efforts of the successful work a second time, hoping to solidify their identity and reputation even more. Once could be an accident, but twice is more assured. But because success can be fickle and fleeting, the insecurity remains.

This insecurity can also cause us to be fearful of changing anything. In fact, it is quite hard to transition from success to another challenge. Transitioning from failure is far easier as we clearly recognize the lessons learned. Once we are successful, in our second endeavor, everything and everyone may be shouting at us to not change a thing. But doing the same thing over and over trying to maintain a level of success is not the same as growing and thriving—it's actually falling into a rut. This makes progress beyond success a very rare feature for those blessed enough to have experienced it once. The attainment of the initial goal can be a death sentence to further development beyond that goal.

There is a way to grow past success, but we must keep our eyes on something beyond that, something bigger. In fact, success should not really be our primary objective—it is short-lived and can be deceptive. We must transition from success to significance by staying focused on becoming a better person and finishing strong. It sometimes takes conflict, confusion, frustration, pain, failure, loneliness, and fear to break us out of that seduction so that we can learn the lessons that will take us beyond our initial achievements. That is what the second journey provided for Paul. It was full of great highs found at the end of the very deep and dark valleys—where the true lessons are often learned most deeply. And these are the lessons that propelled him into his next journey as well.

Paul's Story: The Second Journey

After the obvious success of the first journey, it would have been natural for Paul to attempt to do the same thing the next time. Perhaps that is what Paul might have done—if an unexpected disagreement had not broken up the band.

Conflict: Paul Flies Out on Wings All His Own

At the end of Acts 15, Luke tells us that Paul proposed to Barnabas that they visit all the cities where they had proclaimed the word of the Lord. These two spiritual parents were worried about the welfare of their new Galatian churches. Had the churches received the letter Paul had sent them? Had they responded well to its message?[1] Now that they had the official letter from James and the Jerusalem church council, they were anxious to bring the good news to the churches and, hopefully, settle some of the conflict. But as plans were being made, a sharp disagreement arose between Paul and Barnabas over who should go. There may have been other issues brewing under the surface, but none are mentioned in the text.

Paul did not want John Mark, who had deserted them on the first journey, to accompany him and Barnabas. Paul believed that past behavior is the best predictor of future behavior. Barnabas, however, was of the persuasion that people could change and needed to be given the chance to grow and develop. In the heated debate, I'm sure Barnabas was not shy about using Paul's own story as evidence for his point of view. Their disagreement was so serious that they parted ways. John Mark was the stated reason for the breakup, but there were other potential cracks in the foundation of their partnership.

We can speculate on other possible causes for the division. Paul was undoubtedly disappointed in Barnabas for choosing to dine exclusively with the Jews when the representatives from Jerusalem came to Antioch (Galatians 2:13).[2] Paul also had grown in his leadership gifts on that first journey and now was ready to set the agenda from the very start. Another possible reason weighing on Paul may have been a desire for his partner to also have Roman citizenship so that they could escape some of the beatings like the ones he had had to endure. Barnabas was not a Roman citizen, and Paul would never abandon his teammate in the heat of the battle. When they split ways, Paul chose Silas (who had Roman citizenship) as his next partner, so this could have been on Paul's mind (Acts 16:37), so this could have been on Paul's mind as they went their separate ways.

There is a small chance that Barnabas felt disrespected by the apprentice to whom he had given much humble support and opportunity, although honestly, his track record does not merit this speculation. More than anything, Barnabas seems to have been wired to see the potential in others and to have been particularly gifted at drawing that potential out. He did so with Paul and also with John Mark (Colossians 4:10; 2 Timothy 4:11). He could no sooner deny this impulse than deny the Spirit of God in him. Paul may have been great at preaching the message of Jesus and forming new churches, but Barnabas's gift was equally valuable. To deny it would have been to deny the gifts and the leading of Jesus. Barnabas was as adamant about following God's lead regarding his assessment of people's hearts as Paul was about defending the gospel. Neither backed down, and so a split was inevitable.

Barnabas took John Mark and headed back to Cyprus. Paul chose Silas as his new partner, and together they took the land route toward the Galatian region. In that way they not only divided the team but also the task. Silas was a good choice for Paul because he could represent the Jerusalem church as they took the letter from James abroad. In addition, Silas was a prophet (Acts 15:32), and the prophetic spiritual gift is the best one to pair with the apostolic gift in laying a foundation for the church (Ephesians 2:19-22). As mentioned above, Silas was also a Roman citizen (Acts 16:37), which may have been helpful when they faced inevitable persecutions.

Regardless of the reason for the breakup between Paul and Barnabas, the results were not all bad. Now there were two teams covering twice as much ground and reaching twice as many people. Providentially, this would be the primary lesson of the second journey, but it would not truly be realized until deeper pain made it more obvious. God wanted Paul to shift from a strategy of *addition* to one of *multiplication*, and that lesson would start at the very beginning by multiplying the team. All movements start when one becomes two. When God has something important to teach us, pain is often the vehicle that gets us to recognize and respect the new truth. This is true for all of us, and it was true for Paul as well. Even Jesus had to learn the lessons of obedience through what He suffered (Hebrews 5:8), so it is foolish to think that we get a pass from pain.

On this second journey, Paul took the lead from the start. He chose the team, the route, and the strategy. And now that he was leading, he would improve upon the previous work by doing things differently. The original Galatian churches were weak and vulnerable to being led astray. They had become victims of bigoted and bullying religious leaders, and Paul sought an intentional way of preventing that from happening again.

The first part of Paul's adjusted strategy was to recruit a larger team. Over the course of traveling from Antioch through southern Galatia, past Mysia, and all the way to the coastal city of Troas, he recruited Timothy and Luke, which made this team twice the size of the previous band.[3]

Young Timothy, probably around twenty-one years old at this time, had likely demonstrated strong potential and a heart for the Lord as he shadowed Paul for a time on his previous journey (2 Timothy 3:10-11). But to join in on this next journey, he had to count the cost more than others on the team. Timothy had a Jewish mother, which by canonical law made him a Jew even though his deceased father was Greek. Perhaps his father had objected to circumcision because he saw it as cruel or because he wanted to prevent embarrassment for his boy in the gymnasium. Timothy, having lost his father and been raised by his mother and grandmother (2 Timothy 1:5), was likely yearning for a father figure in his life (Philippians 2:22), and Paul showed great interest in him.

The one hitch in the planned teamwork was that visiting the synagogue in each city was crucial to Paul's strategy, and Timothy, who had not been circumcised as a child, would have been considered an unwelcome apostate Jew. In a move that must have seemed quite contrary to the mission of spreading the news of the Jerusalem council's decision concerning the Gentiles, and especially in light of the letter he had just written to the Galatian churches (Galatians 5:1–6, 6:12–16), Paul stepped into the role of Timothy's father (1 Timothy 1:2; 2 Timothy 1:2) and circumcised him. Because Timothy was Jewish, this was a simple act of obedience to the Old Testament law, and it was not a violation of Paul's own belief that those who were Gentiles did not need to become Jews in order to be followers of Christ. Not only did this strategic act fully restore Timothy as an Israelite in good standing, it also granted him access to the synagogues during the missionary journeys.

At personal cost, Timothy became a member of the missionary band and remained a faithful son to Paul all the rest of their days (Philippians 2:22). I sometimes chuckle at the words of Paul to Timothy, reminding him of the suffering Paul as his spiritual father had to endure to bring the gospel to Timothy's people (2 Timothy 3:10–12), all the while knowing the suffering that Timothy had to go through to bring the gospel to Paul's. At any rate, this young man proved early on that he was willing to count the cost and remain faithful, and those qualities would always characterize his life (Philippians 2:19–23). He passed Paul's test of what made a strong missionary, whereas John Mark had not, at least up to this point in the story.

After visiting and strengthening the churches of the Galatian region and encouraging them with the letter from the Jerusalem council, Paul and his team were finally ready to step into completely unreached territory. The entire world was before them, and the first path was leading to Asia Minor.

Silenced: "Plan A" Rejected

Until this point, Paul was pretty sure of what they were going to do. He was drawn to the great potential of the most influential city in all of Asia—Ephesus. The "A" in Plan A stood for *Asia Minor*. Luke tells us, however, that the Holy Spirit forbade them from speaking the word there.

We have no details of how this prohibition came except that it came from the Holy Spirit. Silas was a mature and experienced prophet, so it is very possible that it came through him. Apostles and prophets are designed to work together in pioneering the church as a multiplying breakout movement. It is ideal when the prophetic role provides spiritual intelligence and navigation that inform apostolic action and authority. This could well have been the case with these two. I'm inclined to think this is what happened, but there are many other ways it could have played out. Paul was often given direction from the Lord, and indeed would receive some once the band arrived in Troas a short time later. All of us can receive messages from God, so it isn't necessary that this guidance had come through Silas. We do not know how God got the message across, but the more compelling question is: *Why?*

Paul's view of the strategic influence of Ephesus and Asia Minor was certainly sound, as would later prove true. The prohibition was only temporary. It was not that God didn't like those people; in fact, it is clear that God had great plans for them. Lydia, the first person to turn to Christ on this second journey, was indeed from Thyatira in Asia Minor (Acts 16:14) but living in Macedonia. It may well have been that the soil in that area was just not quite ready for Paul's message, but I hold a different view. I believe that Paul himself was not ready for the work God had planned there. There was a great work waiting but also a great adversary, and Paul had some lessons to learn before he would be ready for this challenge. Therefore, the second journey would have to take him down another path. I will expand more on the adversary that Paul would ultimately meet in Asia Minor when I look more closely at his third journey.

The prohibition was not to stay out of Asia Minor but not to speak the word there. Ouch! That is, in many ways, worse. Paul was silenced. They really couldn't avoid traveling through that region, but they were clearly forbidden by the Holy Spirit to speak the message there. From all that we know of Paul, this must have been the hardest lesson of obedience yet—to have gone all that way, sent by the Antioch fellowship, with documents endorsing their mission from the Jerusalem leadership, only to have the highest authority in the universe forbid any speaking about Jesus.

Blocked: "Plan B" Also Rejected

Paul, like any other good missionary whose Plan A has been shut down, quickly rallied his team to Plan B, where the "B" stood for *Bithynia*, to the north. They made their way to Mysia and intended to enter this influential northern region. But Acts 16 says the Spirit of Jesus did not permit them to reach Bithynia either. They had been prohibited from preaching during their travels to the south through Asia Minor, and now the Spirit of Jesus let them know that they were not to enter the land to the north.

We do not know how the Spirit was delivering these messages, but it may be at this point that Paul was having silent second thoughts about bringing such a strong prophet along on this trip. That is often the case with apostles who want to get things done, and prophets who want them all done right and only at the leading of the voice of God. This is, of course, all speculation, but if these directions came from Silas the prophet, they certainly proved correct in the end, even if frustrating at the time.

They were unable either to go south or venture north. No right turn, no left turn, and no retreat! Paul and his band kept walking forward until they hit the virtual and physical end of the road in Troas at the edge of Aegean Sea. Paul, possibly feeling like a pinball bouncing from one prohibition to another and forbidden to preach the message that burned in his heart, must have been at wit's end when they landed in Troas. The Holy Spirit had led them to this dead end where they finally completed the team by acquiring Luke.[4]

With no destination in mind but finally having a complete team and the seemingly endless horizon of the sea before them, Paul and the others were primed to finally hear God's guidance. God's ways are unpredictable. Our master plan is always second to our Master's plan. No matter how much we think we have it figured out, in the end we can only wave the white flag and surrender to God's direction if we hope to accomplish anything good. That message alone was worth the long journey to Troas. In the literal dark of night and in the metaphorical darkness of not knowing what God wanted, Paul finally saw God's plan revealed: Plan M, where "M" stood for *Macedonia*. Luke says that a vision came to Paul: "A man of Macedonia was standing and appealing to him, and saying, 'Come over to Macedonia and help us.'"

Imagine the relief Paul and the team felt when they finally got this revelation. They immediately found passage on a ship heading past Samothrace to Neapolis. From darkness to direction, they now knew what they were to do, and everything seemed to fall into place. The frustration and confusion were behind them—and so was a strong wind. In only two days, they made it to their destination (a trip that would take them more than twice as long on the way back). Following the Lord's direction is always much easier than trying to force our own plans to work—not that the rest of Paul's second journey was going to be easy. There was still much for Paul to learn in preparation for the other journeys he would take.

Pain: First Disciples in Europe

After landing in eastern Macedonia, the team walked up to the city of Philippi from Neapolis. Philippi, named after Alexander the Great's father, Philip, was a Roman colony—a little Rome. It was full of Roman pride, Latin was spoken in all official business, and Roman citizenship was held in very high regard. It was also a strategic military post, and so it was full of both active and retired soldiers. This place was very pro-Rome in every way.

Luke says that the team stayed there many days. On his first journey, Paul had normally entered the synagogue after arriving in a new city and preached the message of Christ. Once some people had believed, and others became outraged, he moved on to the next city. But in Philippi, he did things differently. First of all, there was no synagogue, which meant that there were not even ten Jewish men in the whole city.

Paul's pattern was always to preach the gospel first to the Jews. He had clearly defined theological convictions that the good news was to go to the Jews first, then to the Gentiles (Romans 1:16; 2:9,10). This was a group he could relate to on many levels; they were, in a sense, his people, although they did not usually accept him. Like Jesus, he went to his own, and his own did not accept him. Paul, having grown up in a Jewish community in Tarsus, knew how to discover the Jews living in Gentile cities even when there was no synagogue (Acts 16:12–13).

On the first Sabbath, the team went past the northwestern gate and walked down to the Gangites River, hoping to find a place of prayer. There they found a group of God-fearers (Gentiles who believed in Judaism but were not yet proselytes or circumcised) who listened to their message. Lydia from Thyatira was a prominent businesswoman who sold highly valued purple fabrics, and the Lord "opened her heart to respond to the things spoken by Paul." God had earlier prohibited Paul from speaking the message of Jesus in Asia Minor but the first person to receive his gospel message on this second journey was from that very region. This confirms that it wasn't the people or the culture that caused the prohibition. There was something more behind it, seemingly tied to the region's territory.

Lydia and all of her *oikos* (household) were baptized. She invited the team to stay at her home while they were in town, and she would not accept "no" for an answer. Her house became the base for the Philippian mission.

Paul's previous pattern, whether he was chased out of town by persecution or not, had been to leave the new church in the care of the Holy Spirit and move on to the next location (Acts 13:5–6, 12–14; Acts 14:25; Acts 17:33–18:1)—but this time he didn't. The apostles continued walking the streets of Philippi as if they were looking for someone. I believe they were.

In every city of the world there is a syndicate of evil and politically powerful men who get wealthy at the expense of young women, and Philippi was no different. In this case, a demonized slave girl was being exploited for a fortune-telling business that was owned by such wicked men. A strange voice completely beyond her control would come out of her body and predict the future. We can assume that the crafty demons would then arrange circumstances to "fulfill" the predictions, thus preying on the fearful and superstitious nature of the people.

As Paul and his companions roamed the streets, this slave girl would follow them and occasionally shout out in a demonic voice, "These men are bond-servants of the Most High God, who are proclaiming to you the way of salvation." At first Paul just ignored her and went about his business. But her practice of following and shouting at Paul and Silas raised much concern and curiosity among the Philippians, who would have highly respected her spiritual insights as coming from a god. Paul wanted no part of free demonic publicity or of people exploiting this girl, and so he turned and authoritatively cast the demon out of her, setting her free.

The girl's masters who had been using her were outraged at the loss of their business. Paul and Silas were dragged before the authorities and accused of trying to get the good Roman citizens of Philippi to disobey the laws of Rome. It was also noted that Paul and his band were Jews. Just before this time, a law had been passed in the Roman Empire to banish all Jews from Rome. In a place like Philippi, which had no Jews and was a proud Roman colony, these accusations were enough reason for the authorities to beat the apostles publicly with rods and toss them into jail, ignoring the law.

But there was something wrong with this entire scenario. Paul and Silas were both Roman citizens, which would have prevented their being beaten and jailed without a proper trial. Why did Paul not mention their status? It couldn't be that they forgot about it. How many blows would any of us need across our back before remembering that we had a "get out of beating free" card? No, they understood the circumstances and the climate and could easily have flashed their credentials if they had wanted to. We know this because they did exactly that the next day—after the beating. In Philippi, Roman citizenship was very valued and respected (Philippians 3:20–21).[5] So why did they endure a beating when they didn't need to? I believe it was for the same reason that they had not yet moved on from Philippi. They were looking for someone and wouldn't rest until they found him. They had to endure this beating in order to find the path that would lead them to him.

Luke's writing style is always quite precise, but in Acts 16:19–20 he makes a statement that appears to be redundant about the people Paul and Silas were being tried before. It is so out of character that the scholar William Ramsay speculates that Luke never actually finished the manuscript as he would have liked.[6] But we need not doubt the veracity of the Scripture here. Instead, we can ask why Luke would have used two different but almost identical terms to describe who was sentencing them.

One of the terms used was a common Greek expression, but the other term was a more official Roman title for roughly the same type of officer. It may be that the court that first assembled was merely a band of local officials ("the authorities") and that the Roman representatives, including the Roman jailer, then appeared and presided over the trial ("the chief magistrates"). If indeed Luke's language is precise, he must have intended us to ask why he had used both terms. I suggest that the moment the Roman magistrates appeared and took over the proceedings, Paul saw the one he was looking for all along, the man from his vision—the jailer. I believe this is the best answer and is a clue for us to discover why the apostles kept silent about their Roman citizenship and endured the beating.[7] The apostles allowed themselves to be taken along by the Holy Spirit to find the fulfillment of their mission, even when the path took them through difficult circumstances and physical pain.

In any case, after Paul and Silas were beaten, the jailer locked their feet in stocks in the deepest part of the jail. Unable to sleep, the two began to pray and sing praises to the Lord. I imagine the hopeful voices of these undefeated apostles combined with the acoustics of the solid stone walls, ceilings, and floors made for quite a beautiful and soulful worship experience. For whatever reason, those in the jail were so amazed by these two prisoners' sense of peace and freedom that even after a chance for freedom presented itself, they felt compelled to stay.

About midnight, a great earthquake suddenly occurred—and not any ordinary earthquake. As it struck, the chains fell off all the prisoners' wrists and ankles, and the doors swung open. The earthquake awakened the jailer, who grabbed his sword and rushed to check on his charges.

What he had feared lay before him—the doors were wide open, and there was only darkness inside. As a military man, he knew that the only noble recourse for his failure was suicide, as Roman law dictated that if a jailer lost his prisoners, he was to receive the punishment meant for the prisoners. He was about to plunge his blade into his heart when he heard a voice.

I imagine that Paul, inside the jail and looking out through the doorway, saw the moonlit silhouette of a figure drawing his blade. Paul quickly called out, "Do not harm yourself, for we are all here!" The jailer, in frantic hope and nagging unbelief, called for lights from his slaves and found that Paul's words were true—*all* the prisoners had stayed. They had found greater freedom beside Paul, Silas, and their Savior than they would have found in an escape from the jail. The courageous jailer with the sword came trembling in fear before the apostles and dropped to his knees. After he brought them out of their cell he asked, "Sirs, what must I do to be saved?"

What would cause such a response from the jailer and from all the other prisoners? There was much at work in this scenario. God had arranged the whole thing, and Paul and Silas knew it. He had led them to this very moment. The demonized fortune-teller had already spread their reputation as being sent from the Highest God and having the way of salvation. The joyful and unquenchable spirits of Paul and Silas, as they sang in the face of physical pain, were a strong draw for those who were in that jail; the apostles demonstrated that they had stronger than normal faith in their God. The supernatural earthquake (chains falling off and locked doors opening) would have made the superstitious people think that God was not pleased with how his servants were being treated. All of this caused their fellow inmates and the jailer to react in such a highly unusual manner. Fear of the Most High God had come upon them, and they did not choose the alternative of escape, whether by running away or suicide. They all wanted to stay with these servants of God and receive the promised salvation. The wonder and attraction of the Holy Spirit drew them to remain close.

Paul responded to the jailer's request by saying, "Believe in the Lord Jesus, and you will be saved, you and your household [*oikos*]." I used to think that Paul was being prophetic when he announced the salvation of the jailer's entire household, but lately I have come to see this another way. Paul was not speaking prophetically but strategically and confidently, on the basis of previous revelation. The jailer was not just a man of peace whose household would now come to Jesus (Luke 10:1-12), although he was that. I believe he may have actually been the man in Paul's vision in Troas, the Macedonian who called out to Paul: "Come over here and help *us*" (emphasis added).

It bears repeating that this may have been the man Paul and Silas had been searching for all along and the reason they remained in Philippi even after a viable church had been started. That would explain why they endured the seemingly unnecessary pain of being beaten with rods.[8] Paul had traveled hundreds of miles over land and sea to find this man, and he wouldn't have let a beating stop him from accomplishing his mission. It was likely that when the Roman delegation arrived at the haphazard trial, Paul recognized the jailer as the Macedonian man from his vision. Paul confidently knew that the man and his household would all come to Christ because the request in the vision was in the plural, "help us."

There was much rejoicing. The jailer washed their physical wounds, and Paul and Silas symbolically washed away the jailer's sins in baptism, along with those of his entire household—his wife, his children, his slaves and workers—and perhaps even some of the inmates.

In the morning, word came from the Roman political entity (the chief magistrates) via their policemen to let the Jewish prisoners go. The jailer was overjoyed to deliver that message but was shocked when he heard Paul's response. It was at this time that Paul let the policemen know that he and Silas were Roman citizens. When the magistrates heard that the men they had beaten in public and locked in prison were Romans, they became frightened. Their exalted view of Rome was suddenly turned against them. They immediately came to Paul and Silas, brought them out of the prison, and begged them to leave town.

Strategic Shortcomings Discovered: Paul Reaches the End of His Plans

Paul and his companions obliged and left town but not until they visited once more with the church in Lydia's home. And perhaps they were hoping that the fear the city officials felt was enough to secure peace for the new church in their absence. But that wasn't all Paul wanted to do for the church he was leaving. Here we see another change in his previous missionary pattern. Luke stayed behind in Philippi. This is a clue to a second shift in Paul's strategy from the first journey. I believe that Paul had intentionally recruited a larger team so that he would be able to leave workers behind to nurture the young churches through their vulnerable first days without slowing down the progress of the missionary journey. The team would no longer leave behind churches that had no leadership in their impressionable early stages.

In Acts 17, Paul, Silas, and Timothy traveled from Philippi through Amphipolis and Apollonia until they arrived at Thessalonica. There they found a synagogue and stayed three weeks, reasoning from the Scriptures with the Jews about the evidence that Jesus was the Messiah.

Eventually some God-fearers and Gentiles, along with a few Jews, came to believe, and a church was born. Once again strife followed, and it came to a head when a mob pursued Paul and Silas for "turning their world upside down." After the crowd calmed down, the new believers sent the missionaries away by night. Timothy is not mentioned in the departing group. It is possible he stayed behind, following Paul's new strategy.[9]

When they arrived in Berea, Paul and Silas found the Jews there more receptive, but the angry Thessalonians were not content with just having the apostles move on. They came after them to Berea to cause trouble. Many of the people in Berea believed, but the crowds were stirred up once again, and so it was impossible for Paul to stay. A few of the local believers took him farther south all the way to Athens, and Silas was left behind with the new church in Berea, just as Luke had stayed in Philippi and Timothy had remained in Thessalonica.[10]

Paul was now alone without his team. Some plans look good in theory, but in real life they quickly fall apart.

After Paul arrived in Athens and his escort went back to Berea, he realized that his new strategy also was flawed. He was alone—and how would he ever be able to recruit a team large enough to leave representatives behind at each stop?

This may all seem perfectly obvious to us, looking back two thousand years. The reality, however, is that most of us try to recruit people to fill needs in much the same way, and our own strategies meet the same dead-end results. Whenever we attempt to mobilize folks to fill in gaps in our strategies, we inevitably find that there are more roles to be handled than there are people to fill them. We should keep this in mind before we conclude that Paul was foolish for attempting what we have all done so often.

Loneliness In Athens

I think it was very hard for Paul to be alone once again after his years in Tarsus. He didn't seem to do well alone, and even in solitary confinement while on death row in Rome he said, "Luke is with me" (2 Timothy 4:11). Talk about a faithful companion! There are not many who get to have a friend with them in the dungeon, nor are there many friends who would oblige.

But at this juncture near the end of his strategy on his second journey, Paul found himself alone in a foreign city full of demonic idols. It was said that there were more statues of gods in Athens than all of Greece combined and you were more likely to meet a god there than a person.[11] Luke says that he was "provoked" by the idolatry he witnessed. He was extremely upset. The openly demonic oppression he saw in this city was eating him up from deep within.[12] He was motivated to speak the word of God and try to reason with the people for as long as he could endure.

The glory that once was Greece had by now faded under the bright lights of Rome. Athens was long past her glory days as the global center of cultural and philosophical advancement. Luke comments that the people, perhaps still longing for the good old days, had nothing better to do with their time "than telling or hearing something new." Paul was glad to oblige by reasoning every day with the people in the synagogue and the marketplace. The Epicurean and Stoic philosophers wanted to hear more, and so they invited him to speak at the Areopagus. The Areopagus, sometimes called Mars Hill, was a large rock where ideas and disputes were shared, discussed, and occasionally settled. It was here that Socrates met his accusers, but by the time Paul was taken to this historic site, much of the authority of the court had been diminished, and so at that time they evaluated issues of education and general matters related to the marketplace.[13]

When Paul spoke to the philosophers on Mars Hill, he presented a masterful sermon—short and to the point, with illustrations from his audience's common experience as well as quotes from some of their own prized literature. Paul is well past emulating Stephen—he now has his own brilliant voice.

Although Paul later authored the great poem of true love in 1 Corinthians 13, which is often read at wedding ceremonies, this is how he described himself on this second journey: "I did not come in superiority of speech or of wisdom" (1 Corinthians 2:1). Those who questioned Paul's authority to the Corinthians claimed that Paul's writings were strong but his speech was contemptible and his appearance unimpressive (2 Corinthians 10:10). Maybe those things were true, but this sermon demonstrates that he was indeed a man of great oratory abilities when empowered by the Holy Spirit and speaking about what he loved most in life.

After his brief message, some of his audience believed, but most did not. Paul did not stay in Athens much longer. Perhaps he was so agitated by the city's idolatry—a provocation accentuated by his own sense of loneliness—that he left the new church behind and went to Corinth.

Fear In Corinth

In many respects, Corinth was the sin capital of the world. It had a quarter of a million people jammed into a relatively small place and was the largest city (apart from Antioch) that Paul had encountered on his missionary journeys so far. It sat on a strategic isthmus, the narrow bridge of land connecting the much larger landmasses of Macedonia and Achaia. As a result, Corinth was at a crossroads, with travelers coming from every direction, by land and by sea, with two ports, one on each side; it also had two markets to sell the cargo dropped off there.

Try to imagine what the city must have looked like when all the sailors and their cargo, legal and illegal, got off at one place. To add to this environment, Corinth was most famous for its temple of worship for the goddess Aphrodite. This cult was dedicated to glorifying sex, with a thousand temple prostitutes devoted to that purpose.

Paul, alone in a sea of people and sin, was afraid. The idolatry in Athens provoked him, but the blatant and wanton sinfulness of Corinth had a different effect—he was frightened. It is hard for us who read the New Testament to ever think that the great apostle Paul was afraid of anything, but he was. Later he wrote to the Corinthians, "I was with you in weakness and in *fear* and in *much trembling*" (1 Corinthians 2:3, emphasis added). We might consider this hyperbole from a humble apostle, but there is one other witness who verified his fear. One night, while Paul was alone and afraid, Jesus came to him in a vision and said, "*Do not be afraid any longer*, but go on speaking and do not be silent; for I am with you, and no man will attack you in order to harm you, for I have many people in this city" (Acts 18:9–10, emphasis added).

These words from Jesus were not simply comforting words to strengthen Paul's resolve in the face of his immediate fears. As we will discover below, these words from Jesus spoke to all the pain and the hardships Paul endured throughout this journey. Like Paul, we may experience suffering, brush it off, and get back to work, but Jesus never forgets our struggles. He remembers every tear even if we have long moved on from the experience that caused it (Psalm 56:8; Revelation 21:4).

The Lesson Learned: Jesus' Plan is Better than All Others

Jesus also revealed a major upgrade to Paul's missionary strategy in the Corinthian vision. This message would alter Paul's missionary endeavors in permanent and powerful ways.

Until this moment Paul's strategy had been to go to a town, win as many disciples as possible starting with the Jews, and then move on to the next place to do it all again. On this second journey, presumably having seen the weakness of the Galatian churches, he altered his methodology by recruiting more leaders and leaving them behind to oversee the young churches while he went to the next town. But this plan also was less effective than he desired. It was when Paul was in this weak and broken state that Jesus stepped in to give him a new strategy, one that would eventually reach the entire Gentile world and change history. For most of us, we are less inclined to listen and learn when we are feeling strong. When we are broken down in weakness, then we learn the most. Paul was ready to learn.

This short message directly from the Lord of the harvest spoke to everything Paul needed to hear. Every difficulty he faced on this journey—

his silencing in Asia, his being blocked in Bithynia, his physical pain in Philippi, his loneliness in Athens, his fear in Corinth, and even his shortsighted strategy throughout—is addressed by Jesus in a simple and straightforward message.

To Paul's fear Jesus said, "Do not be afraid." To his pain Jesus said, "No man will attack you to hurt you." To his loneliness Jesus said, "I am with you." Where he once was silenced, now Jesus said, "Do not be silent." Where he once was blocked, Jesus said, "Go on speaking." And to Paul's shortsighted strategy Jesus said, "I have many people in this place."

In other words: "Find your team here among these sinful people; don't wait for Silas and Timothy to come." Jesus addressed every one of Paul's hardships with this powerful and comforting word, which I'm sure touched Paul deep in his heart and strengthened him beyond imagination.

In essence, Jesus strategically instructed Paul not to leave so quickly. Rather than recruiting and importing a team from another place, *he was to find his coworkers in the harvest fields.*

I believe that it was at this time that Paul sought to find a place to put his professional training of making tents into practice.[14] After hearing from Jesus, Paul permanently changed his approach to mission and stayed in Corinth, which was a good place to be a tentmaker. With its large population, its two bustling marketplaces, and its location as the site of the periodically held Isthmian Games, Corinth always needed more tents.[15]

In his vocational work, Paul met Aquila and Priscilla, who had been forced out of Rome because they were Jewish. Paul had much in common with this couple, and so he joined them in trade and living. Luke then tells us that Paul set out to reason daily in the synagogues with the Jews. Aquila and Priscilla joined him and followed Jesus.[16] Paul found new team members who would work with him throughout his life right where Jesus said he would—within the harvest fields. Aquila and Priscilla were only the start; there would be many more, including Crispus (the leader of the synagogue) and the well-respected Titius Justus, who hosted the new church in his home next door to the synagogue.

Acts tells us that Paul stayed about eighteen months in Corinth after he heard from Jesus, a clear indication of a dramatic change in his strategic approach to the mission. A year and a half was a long time to stay in one place for a man who had traveled 1,500 miles in one year on his previous journey. Paul's methods were shifting from a strategy of addition to one of multiplication. He would no longer just add disciples to the church but would raise workers from the harvest in order to multiply the influence of Christ's word over entire regions and ultimately over the Roman Empire.

After his work was done in Corinth and threats began to mount against him, Paul did the sensible thing—*he stayed longer*. I believe that in part this was not because the work needed him but because Jesus told him personally that no harm would come to him there. Paul chose to put his faith in Jesus' words and prove them true instead of letting the circumstances around him dictate his agenda. Fear was no longer an issue. Jesus took care of that and much more. Of course, Jesus' words were faithful and true. No harm came to Paul in Corinth.

The Return Trip

After enough time had passed to prove his point, Paul set sail for Syria, accompanied by Aquila and Priscilla. When they reached Ephesus, Paul went to the synagogue and reasoned with the Jews, but only for a little while. As soon as he saw that they were receptive and wanted him to stay longer, he again did the sensible thing—*he left*. Why?

I believe he wanted to test whether the prohibition against speaking in Asia Minor had been lifted after he learned the lessons of the second journey. The Holy Spirit had forbidden him to speak in Asia, but not to Asians (Lydia in Philippi was Asian). It appears that the restriction had been lifted, and so he was hoping to return but not planning for it. He had learned well, and so he said, "I will return to you again *if God wills*" (Acts 18:21, emphasis added). It appears that he just dipped his toes in the water of Asia Minor to see if it was safe to jump in, left Aquila and Priscilla there, and then set off first for Jerusalem and then for home, in Antioch.

This was his longest recorded sea voyage—Ephesus to Caesarea. Luke is meticulous about mentioning by name the many ports that the apostles came to on their sea journeys. The text implies that Paul visited the Jerusalem church briefly before he made his way back to his home base in Antioch. He did not stay long,[17] although he picked up a new task. After visiting Jerusalem, he took up the task of raising a gift for the poor in the church there.

Multiplication: Evidence of a Lesson Learned and Better Things to Come

Before we move on, it is interesting that at this point Luke takes off on what initially looks like a tangent in his narrative. In Acts 18:24–28, Luke tells us about some events that took place in Ephesus and beyond. Beginning in Acts 13, Luke's narrative focuses solely on Paul. There is no further mention of Peter or Barnabas, and after Acts 18:5 Luke doesn't even include Silas or Timothy by name in the story. But for some reason, Luke launches into the story of a new character—Apollos.

Apollos was an Alexandrian Jew who was a great orator and a master of the Old Testament Scriptures. Apollos was acquainted with John the Baptist and knew of Jesus only through that lens. Priscilla and Aquila had heard him in the synagogue of Ephesus and were greatly impressed but noticed that he didn't have the whole story yet. Therefore, they met with him privately and explained the fullness of the gospel, including the death, burial, and resurrection of Jesus and the baptism of faith.[18] Apollos gladly received this more complete explanation and immediately wanted to go out to share the news with others. The church wrote him a letter commending him to the brothers and sisters in Achaia, and off he went. Luke says he helped the church in many ways and was powerful in refuting "the Jews in public, demonstrating by the Scriptures that Jesus was the Christ" (Acts 18:28).

Why would Luke, with his already full parchment, pause his account of Paul's mission and take space to introduce this person?[19] It is my belief that this is not a tangent but rather a magnifying glass, letting us look more closely at the results of the lesson Jesus taught Paul in Corinth on this second journey. Luke is showing us the effects of multiplying leadership from the harvest to the fourth generation. To do this absolutely requires the author to venture away from Paul, even if for only a few sentences. Multiplication is only possible if the movement of disciples goes far beyond the initial catalyst who begins it.

Paul found Aquila and Priscilla in the harvest and taught them the truths of the gospel while reasoning in the synagogue about the evidence of Jesus as Messiah. Then this couple found Apollos and did the same with him. The paragraph ends with Apollos in turn doing the same, using language very similar to the language that describes Paul's ministry to the Jews (Acts 17:2–3). At this point, Apollos had not yet met Paul, but he was reproducing his methodology effectively because Paul had multiplied himself.

Compare the language Luke uses to describe Paul's evangelistic method with the language he uses for that of Apollos:

LUKE'S ACCOUNT OF PAUL'S EVANGELISTIC METHOD	LUKE'S ACCOUNT OF APOLLOS' EVANGELISTIC METHOD
" . . . and according to Paul's custom he [Paul]	" . . . he [Apollos]
went to them [the Jews]	powerfully refuted the Jews
and for three Sabbaths	in public
reasoned with them from the Scriptures	demonstrating by the Scriptures
saying, 'This Jesus whom I am proclaiming to you is the Christ'" (Acts 17:2–3).	that Jesus was the Christ" (Acts 18:28).

Though my assumptions in this passage are theoretical and differ from most commentators, the observed outcomes do substantiate my interpretations. In my opinion, these observations of Paul's experiences and the lessons he learned make the most sense of Luke's narrative. He did change his strategy on the basis of Jesus' words. He found workers in the city, and they began to multiply, beginning with Priscilla and Aquila and then going on to Apollos and beyond. From this point on, Paul's strategy was no longer that of an itinerant. He stayed in one place longer, raised disciples from the harvest, trained them on the job, and sent them out as self-sufficient missionaries. His work shifted from merely adding to God's Kingdom to multiplication movements with exponential growth thereafter. Jesus' ideas are always better than our own.

Your Story: Lessons of the Second Journey

The apostle Paul is, indeed, a special man in history. I do not believe it is because of his training, spiritual giftedness, personality, or background, but because he was so open to the work God wanted to do in his life—both through him and in him. Do not forget that. Paul is consistently put forth for us as an example of someone we can and should follow (Philippians 3:17; 2 Timothy 1:13, 2:2; 1 Corinthians 4:16–17, 11:1). It is important that we recognize the many shared aspects between his life development and our own. Any of us—all of us—have as much access to Almighty God as Paul—we just need the same willingness to follow Him. There are reasons that we do not follow as readily, and I suggest that our low pain-tolerance level is indeed an impediment to following as closely as Paul did. On his second trip, Paul's journey into Christlikeness led him through many of the learning cycles that we all must experience if we hope to finish well, and they were all experienced in the midst of pain and discomfort.

Breaking with a Mentor—and Coming Back

At a critical point in Paul's development, he had a falling-out with Barnabas, his mentor and friend. Dr. Charles Ridley, an expert in the assessment of church planters, founded his evaluation method on a simple idea: the best predictor of future behavior is past behavior. It appears that Paul held closely to the same philosophy regarding John Mark. Barnabas, by contrast, was quite familiar with the potential and power of a changed life, as amply demonstrated by his confidence in Paul's conversion and transformation. Barnabas was a mentor comfortable with giving and receiving second chances.

Having been given so much freedom to experiment on his first journey, Paul was now confident that he knew what was necessary to conduct the mission correctly the second time around, and he was not going to repeat what he felt were the team's previous missteps. This meant that Paul was not going to give John Mark a second chance.

On second journeys, emerging leaders who step out to do things their own way often show a sudden decrease in respect for their mentors. This phase usually lasts about a year and has been called *adolescent rebellion syndrome* (ARS). This syndrome is often about methodology and philosophy of ministry. It is a result of the power dynamics that come with the transition of roles. My mentor Ralph Moore first observed this phenomenon and coined the ARS term. Ralph founded the Hope Chapel movement, (which has thousands of churches all over the world) and has sent out more church planters in a Western context than anyone else I know. Therefore, it was God's grace that I had a chance to chat with Ralph when I was experiencing a nightmare of rejection by a beloved friend I had been coaching. Ralph smiled and told me that ARS occurs when an emerging leader is suddenly given the role of primary leader and steps out of the shadow of his mentor. In the second-journey leaders' mind, this is their chance to do things better, so they are not open to their mentors' input and instead put into place ideas that represent their own strategic plans.

I am so grateful for those fifteen minutes during a car ride with Ralph. That conversation has borne much fruit in my life. Ralph described exactly what I had been experiencing with people I was mentoring. His words of outstanding advice were something like this: "When the emerging leader suddenly has no respect for you, do not get offended and retaliate with defensiveness or a lack of respect in return. Be the grown-up. Just as a parent will love their own child through any rebellion, you must show love, support, and compassion even in the face of rejection. This is very much like Jesus, who faced the vilest rebellion from the loved ones he trained. He was betrayed, abandoned, and denied by his apprentices, yet his love for them never diminished." After Ralph let this truth seep in, he added even more wisdom gained from his years of experience. He told me that when a mentor loves an apprentice through the phase of ARS, within a year the apprentice will come back, usually in tears, and the relationship will be restored and can even become deeper. If the mentor reacts to ARS by rejecting the apprentice, the relationship may never be restored. Then he emphasized, "Remain the parent in the relationship. One of you has to be the grownup. Don't be childish."

While Paul and Barnabas were back in Antioch after their first journey, there was a lot of tension. The first fissure in their relationship probably occurred when Barnabas pulled away from dining with the Gentiles in

Antioch (Galatians 2:11–13). That could well have been the start of Paul's lack of respect, which developed into a full-blown case of ARS. Then they had a methodological disagreement over who should be on the team for the next journey, which led to them leading separate teams.

Three or four years after they parted company, Paul wrote a letter to the Corinthian church. In it he mentions Barnabas in very flattering terms (1 Corinthians 9:6). This is important because as we have seen, the Corinthian church was initiated on Paul's second journey after he split up with Barnabas. The Corinthians would be familiar with Silas and Timothy but not Barnabas. I believe this is an indication that the relationship between Paul and Barnabas was healed and restored even if the partnership was not. Paul later went on to comment that John Mark was useful in a missionary context (2 Timothy 4:11), voicing his recognition that Barnabas was right. ARS is never meant to be a permanent condition. In fact, in my own experience, the better you have been as a mentor, the more likely you will experience this rejection. Why? Because it really only happens when you grant empowerment to the second-journey leader. As a good mentor steps out of the way, the younger leader wants to try new things and do them differently, like Paul did. Barnabas was a good mentor.

Paul had to mature, just as we all do. We cannot be faulted for being at the level of maturity that is natural in our progression. The problem lies in *not* progressing. We may applaud the off-balance first steps of children when they are less than a year old. When ten-year-olds stagger the same way, we know that something is not right. Paul would be more mature on his later journeys, but that does not mean he was wrong to have the characteristics of a second-journey person at this time. The same is true for each of us. It is not bad to go through the growing pains of the second journey—it is bad to remain stuck and not move on to the next one.

Learning to Surrender to God's Plan

Just as Paul had to scrap both his Plan A and Plan B, second-journey people often find that their plans—no matter how good—are not God's plans. The more quickly they develop their intimacy with God and learn to listen and follow, the better off they will be. It is at this stage of development that leaders must surrender to the Lord of the harvest and let go of all the plans that seem so perfect in their heads.

God never downloads the whole plan at once; we must discover it along the way. This is because *the greater goal is not that we accomplish something but that we grow more intimate with our Lord.* Those who listen well to God will find that God listens well to them, and they will accomplish a lot more.

In the 1990s, I served as regional director of church planting for my denomination. I received many church-planting proposals from eager second-journey leaders. Some were outstanding, some were not. Nevertheless, I never saw any of those proposals fulfilled as originally planned. Not one. Not even the best of them. God doesn't want us to feel as if we can do this on our own, nor does He want us to feel that it is our place to plan how His church is started or built. Jesus specifically said, "*I* will build *my* church" (Matthew 16:18, emphasis added).

About a year after my first church plant (while I was still functioning as director of church planting), I received a proposal from Brad Fieldhouse, a young leader I had been mentoring. He had just finished his master's degree and taken a class where he developed a church-planting proposal under the tutelage of my own mentor, Bob Logan. He received a good grade and turned it in to his denominational leaders, who were very excited about it and wanted to support him. Finally, he presented it to me in my office. The document, spiral bound, was almost an inch thick.

Brad later described our meeting in this way: "I handed Neil the proposal, and he said, 'Thanks' and immediately turned and dropped it in the trash can beside his desk. Shocked and confused, I said, 'If you don't have time for it, I will understand.'"

I replied, "No, I have time. I just don't want to read it right now." After a pause and a sly smile, I went on to say, "More importantly, I want you to be free of it. You see, we know that church-planting proposals never describe what actually happens. I have seen dozens of these proposals. What I have never seen is a single one carried out as planned. The value of the exercise is to see that you can think strategically, and I already know that about you, Brad. What is in this proposal and what is out there on the streets will be very different, and the sooner you realize it, the freer you will be. That is why I just threw your hard work in the trash. I did it for you."[20]

Brad later said that this was the most helpful advice he received before he began to start churches. After our conversation, I took his proposal out of the trash and put it on my reading pile. I had wanted to make a point to Brad, and he got it.

The network of organic churches Brad started, called CrossRoads, did not look much like the church he originally envisioned in his game plan. After starting those churches, he went on to launch a city transformation ministry called Kingdom Causes, which continues to make a difference in urban areas to this day. Then he built an NGO called City Net that helps reduce homelessness and human trafficking. He now manages hundreds of employees working all across the state of California. While seed thoughts about some of these ideas were in his original proposal, none of these initiatives were there. Brad has discovered God's plan as he followed Jesus into the fields.

It is not bad to have a plan; it is bad to be cemented to our plan, without flexibility. A strategic thinker who listens closely to the Lord of the harvest is a powerful agent in God's Kingdom. It is far better to have a strategic mind and a willing heart than a strategic plan and willing donors.

Second-journey people must learn to overcome their success, which can actually be a greater challenge than overcoming their failures. We must be willing to kill our darling plans and methods if we hope to find better ones. Sometimes a very good plan is the enemy of the best one.

Paul's original plan involved recruiting a highly qualified team to accomplish more ministry. In fact, he rejected some gifted leaders in the process, because he wanted only the best. Does that sound familiar? That's what almost all Christian leaders do. The problem he ran into is that this approach has a low ceiling for growth. It doesn't take long to discover there are more needs than there are team members to fill them. Recruitment is always a dead end.

Jesus' plan was better. He wanted Paul to discover all the team members he would ever need in the harvest itself…and multiply. Paul's plan was merely addition. Jesus' plan, multiplication, could go to scale with all the needs found in the world and never hit the ceiling. It is not as hard to abandon the old plan when we realize the greatness of Jesus' plan.

The Gift of Suffering

In the coastal town of Troas, Paul had added Luke to his team and finally received the marching orders from his Lord that he desired. They set sail for Philippi and had the wind at their back, but it would not be all smooth sailing. Paul discovered on the second journey that God's plan involved conflict, squelched plans, pain, loneliness, frustration, and fear in its fulfillment.

Why is it that God has us endure pain to fulfill His plan for our lives? The New Testament provides lots of good answers to this question. Here are ten reasons we are allowed to experience pain during our spiritual formation:

1. God loves us, and so He disciplines us. Selfish actions are incredibly destructive. We need to understand, not just cognitively but also experientially, that they have broad and negative consequences—for us and those who love us (Hebrews 12:4–11).
2. The world, the flesh, and the devil hate Jesus, and so they hate us (John 15:18–25; 2 Timothy 3:10–12; 1 Peter 5:8–10) and do all they can to destroy us. Persecution is for all who desire to live godly in Christ Jesus.
3. God wants to get our attention, and sometimes He has to bring us to the point where we are able to listen and learn. Some things are truly learned only when accompanied by hurt. The pain solidifies the lesson in deep places in our lives (Hebrews 5:7–9; 1 Peter 5:8–10).
4. God prepares us for greater fruitfulness by making space for more of Him in our lives. It takes loss to find gain. Suffering teaches us Christlike character. Only when we rid ourselves of lesser supports do we develop a desperate dependence on Him (John 15:1–11; 1 Peter 4:1–3; James 1:2–4). God sometimes takes away things that we depend on so that we lean only on Him.
5. The gospel is truly worth dying for, and suffering demonstrates that—to us and to those around us (Hebrews 12:1,2).
6. Suffering can draw out and display the goodness in us and prove—to God, ourselves, and the world—that we are truly His followers.

In this way, we can be a witness of His love in a context that magnifies His love in a compelling way (Matthew 5:10–12; 2 Timothy 1:7–11; 2 Timothy 2:2–10; 1 Peter 2:18–20, 3:14–17).

7. God permits us to suffer so that we can have fellowship with Christ and know Him even in His suffering (Philippians 1:29, 3:10–11; John 15:18; Romans 8:17; Colossians 1:24; 1 Peter 2:21, 4:12–19). There are parts of Jesus that we cannot know until we have suffered. Let that sink in for a moment.

8. In this fallen world, our suffering prepares us to come to the aid and understanding of those who also suffer (Hebrews 2:17–18; 2 Corinthians 1:3–11). In suffering we are being schooled to care for others.

9. We learn the love and comfort of our salvation when we realize the pain and suffering of this life. We begin to understand the price Jesus paid and to value the gift all the more because of the pain we have experienced in this cursed world, and we have more hope for the life that is to come (Romans 8:16–39). We simply cannot understand the profound goodness of comfort until we have a need to be comforted. Then we discover how unique Jesus truly is.

10. In order to build us into the image of Jesus, God has to break down the old form of ourselves that is preventing us from moving toward that goal (2 Corinthians 4:11-12; Ephesians 4:22-24; 1 Peter 5:10). Losing ourselves is not easy, but it is necessary for us to be like Jesus.

All these answers are true, but they all fall short of satisfying the real heart (and hurt) behind the question. Perhaps the worst thing we could ever do is simply read this list of answers to someone who has suffered great loss. Only the Lord, the God of all comfort, can show us how to suffer well and help others who are experiencing deep pain and loss. Greater minds than mine have addressed this subject more fully than space will allow, so I point you to them.[21]

Ultimately, it may be best to simply realize that pain is not abnormal for the Christian or a detour away from what God has in store for the faithful. Pain is actually the pathway for all godliness. We simply cannot become like the suffering Servant without suffering. If Jesus Himself had to learn obedience with suffering (Heb 5:7-9), how much more do we?

We should also never assume that we are in pain because God has left us or is angry with us. He may discipline us as His children, but it is because of His love, and it is for our own good. But suffering happens for many more reasons than discipline. It was President Theodore Roosevelt who said, "Never throughout history has a man who lived a life of ease left a name worth remembering." Hardship is what makes the story of our lives more compelling in the telling. A story without conflict is one not worth repeating.

The lesson for maturing Christ-followers is to not be surprised when we encounter pain. Because the Scriptures are true in telling us that we will experience suffering, we should be concerned if we do not face difficult challenges and pain. Whom the Lord loves, He disciplines (Hebrews 12:7–11). It is those who are bearing fruit that He prunes, not as punishment but as an investment for them to bear greater fruit in the future (John 15:1–2). He tests the faith of His followers to develop perseverance and joy (James 1:2–4). As a second-journey person, the path to know His love and to bear much fruit, as well as to have greater perseverance and joy, requires hardships.

God doesn't test us because He doesn't know the answer of how we will respond, but because we don't. We really don't know what is in us when we have Christ. The deepest and longest lasting lessons are not learned in a book but through trials and suffering. Learning is a pain, but it's worth it in the end.

Listening in a Season of Aloneness and Fear

After Paul landed in Athens and his guides left him, he realized one of the shortcomings of his adjusted strategy—there were a limited number of times he could leave a team member with a new church before he ran out of companions. Even in a city full of people, noise, and activity, it's not uncommon to feel alone—and Paul did. As we mature in our walks with God, there is often a need to be isolated for a time. In Paul's case, it wasn't the sort of extended isolation that he had endured in Tarsus. It was a brief time of loneliness, just enough to get his attention and communicate a new profound truth. In a real sense, there are many moments when God is speaking, but the noise in our busy lives is too loud for us to really hear and understand. It is at those times that God may intentionally turn down the volume of other voices, including our own, just so we can have ears to hear what He has to say. This enforced, temporary disengagement may seem to happen mainly when we have difficult challenges that cause us to stop, look, and listen.

The time when Paul was alone in Corinth and experiencing deep fear also opened the space for the Lord to appear and speak to him to strengthen his whole being and provide him with a new perspective on how to approach his ministry. It is usually when we reach the end of our own strategies that God shows us a better way. When we hear God's voice at such a time, it does more than simply show us a superior path. It strengthens and empowers us from within and even bestows a new authority on our lives. As hard as it is to hear, there is no doubt that we are all better learners when we face the painful shortcomings of our own strategies.

The second journey typically is not just about refining strategy, although refinement is needed. And it isn't just about developing character, but character is certainly developed. It is a both/and struggle and even more. When we make the Christian experience only about character, we can mistakenly think that what we do doesn't matter—but it does. When we make the Christian life only about methodology and practice, it loses all life and power. Of course, character is the foundation from which methodology has its impact. We can preach beyond our character (and many people do), but we cannot serve as a disciple beyond our character. We can truly go only as far in our spiritual journey as our character will allow. Godliness in character fills the methodology with breath and a beating heart. I believe, however, that we must be open to the fact that God does not simply want to change our hearts but may also, in the process, want to teach us how to better do His work. We must be open to learning and growing in both character and skills.

If a lesson is never truly learned and internalized, we can get caught in the cycle of repeatedly experiencing similar painful challenges. It is one of the ways we can hit a plateau and fall short of finishing well. The pain gets increasingly unbearable, until finally we quit and opt for a supposedly easier life—but that means we become less able to hear God's voice. We would then live out our lives absorbed in the machinations of service, devoid of the spark of life that comes when God's voice and leading are heard. Don't let that happen. The outer veneer of religion is nothing to compare with the inner flames of His constant presence.

The person who walks through and comes out of the second journey is changed. There is an authority that comes from the deep experience of going through the pain, conflict, loneliness, and fear that forms a different person. This authority cannot be faked, and it cannot be acquired by lesser experiences or the mere accumulation of knowledge. Its cost is high because its value is worthy of it.

This change is seen in how Paul responded toward both hostility and hospitality at the end of his second journey. When hostility and threats rose against him in Corinth, he stayed longer instead of leaving. He had faith in the promise of God that rose above all circumstances and so demonstrated his increased authority. Later in Ephesus, people wanted him to stay, but he left. He had elevated his authority to a level that was uncommon and surely remarkable. Other people's opinions had no real leverage over his actions.

Paul's intimacy and faith in Christ dictated his choices rather than the threats or promises of people. With that kind of resolve comes an air of power and confidence that others recognize. Those who come through the second journey are no longer overly swayed by the opinions of others. Popularity is no longer an issue. This is the kind of spiritual authority that flows from the life of someone who has come out of his or her second journey.

 **Second-Journey Reflections**

Here are some practical ideas for people on their second journey:

1. Hold very lightly to your plans and strategies. In fact, I often suggest that new workers take their proposed plans and have a time where they offer them up literally in a bonfire and ask God to lead them into the new work out in the field. How sad it is when I encounter people who have been hard at work for years and who are not open to veering away at all from whatever plans they initially developed. Sadly, some people, to their own detriment and that of all who join them, cling to their plans more tightly than they cling to the imminent and intimate presence of Jesus.

2. Recognize that suffering is part of God's plan, and that you won't be spared just because you are His beloved child. In fact, it is His love that gives you this gift. Suffering does not have to be desired, but it should never be a surprise.

3. Don't take a cheap route. Shortcuts in character formation result in shortcomings in character. Trying to avoid pain can actually take you off the path God has for you. It is better to move forward into what God has for you than to relieve your pain for a moment. It is the desire to escape pain in life that leads many people into all sorts of complacency. Escape is not the solution—endurance is. The fear of further pain can keep you from further learning. It is far better to discover God's grace in the midst of suffering than to avoid suffering entirely.

4. Don't let the lessons learned from the pain become the sole platform of your life and a distraction that prevents the next journey. Rejoice in the lessons learned, but keep on learning. Never be content to remain in your current state. Keep pressing forward.

Here are reflection questions to help you evaluate your journey:

- How have you tried to improve methods over those of your mentors? Did your mentor applaud this or denounce it? How did you respond to your mentor?
- Have you had plans that were completely nullified by God? How quickly were you able to adjust and move on? Can you identify lessons that you might have learned more quickly if you had not stubbornly pursued your own way rather than listening to God?
- Can you identify moments when you chose personal sacrifice, even pain, for the sake of the greater mission? Try to explain the lessons that forced you to abandon one strategy and embrace a new one that turned out to be much improved. How did you discover that?
- Have you found yourself alone on mission with no one but God? Was He enough? What did He do for you in that hard time? Can you identify ways that you faced your fears and found great learning and effectiveness as a result?

As we have seen, the lessons of the second journey are learned through conflict, frustration, pain, mistakes, loneliness, and fear. You can't skip the second journey and hope to finish well. When you pass through the lessons of the second journey, a whole new journey awaits, one of greater and more expansive influence than you can imagine.

CHAPTER 5

THE THIRD JOURNEY

Everything Comes Together

> *Try not to become a man of success but rather to become*
> *a man of value.*
> —Albert Einstein

> *A wide door for effective service has opened to me,*
> *and there are many adversaries.*
> —The apostle Paul describing his third journey (1 Cor. 16:9)

There is a moment in the lives of some people when all their training, experience, learning, character formation, calling, and giftedness align to become one force, resulting in explosive and extensive productivity. J. Robert Clinton refers to this phase of spiritual formation as *convergence*. During convergence, he says, "God moves a leader into a role that matches his or her gift-mix and experience so that ministry is maximized."[1]

Not every person has the privilege of experiencing this phase of life. Some people do not live long enough to reach convergence. Because of the high cost of character formation, many people give up on the growth process in earlier phases of development and simply live out their lives in less fruitful stages of maturity. But those who pay the price and continue until they reach this point become highly effective, with expanding influence. Our greatest significance is waiting at the end of much pain and many hard lessons. No one who truly influences the world in a positive and lasting way over the course of a lifetime does so effortlessly.

It is important to mention that influence and fame are not the same. We can grow into great significance and yet remain obscure. Of course it is probable that some will notice the high impact a third-journey leader exerts, but there are less popular fields of influence. Do not confuse influence with fame or popularity.

Once men and women step into the convergence of the third journey, they will recognize that all their previous journeys were preparation for such a time. To reach a peak in our success earlier in life is in some ways a tragedy of missed opportunity. All of us desire success throughout our lives, but I believe we should aspire to see even greater significance later in life. Success, in and of itself, is a heavy burden to bear; to bear it without a firm foundation of maturity and strong character can lead to great destruction. Achievement built simply on talent, in the absence of the necessary substance of true, hard-won character, will always be short-lived and does not lead to personal fulfillment.

Moses, Daniel, Joseph, John the Baptist, Paul, and especially Jesus, are all familiar to Christians today, but each had many years of which we know little, except that these men were marginalized and unknown. The fact that events of those years were not recorded doesn't mean that they weren't full of important learning. What we learn in the quiet years is often the essential foundation for our more influential years to come.

Paul was willing to pay the price in the present for greater impact in the future, and that was a wise choice. In the city of Ephesus, he stepped into the convergence of all his life's journeys to find his spiritual authority, skill, and character all magnified in an extraordinary way. His resulting powerful influence did not come simply from a new strategy or a new method. It is the return on the investment of hard work and painful struggle. There is a reward that awaits those who are willing to hold firm to Jesus through the challenges of earlier journeys. Convergence is rare and valuable, and that it why it costs so much.

Paul's Story: The Third Journey

Having learned the hard lessons of the second journey, and no longer forbidden by the Holy Spirit to preach the message in Asia Minor, Paul was now ready to go to Ephesus.

The text does not say that Paul had a partner with him on this journey. We are left to guess where Silas was deployed. We can assume that Barnabas was off on his own adventure. Paul, after passing through the Galatian region yet again (a fourth time) to strengthen the disciples there (Acts 18:23), headed straight to Ephesus. This was the most influential city in Asia Minor. There he met up with apprentices he had picked up on his second missionary journey (Acts 19:22, 29).

On his first journey, Paul covered about 1,500 miles in one year. On this third journey, he lived exclusively in Ephesus for three years (Acts 20:31), but the Word of God spread in an incredible way to cover more than 4,000 square miles. In fact, the success of this missionary journey is hard to fathom. Luke says that "all who lived in Asia heard the word of the Lord, both Jews and Greeks" (Acts 19:10). That is an incredibly fruitful mission trip in only three years, especially when there is no record that Paul ever even ventured out of the city of Ephesus. How did he do it?

The Acts of the Holy Spirit

Paul arrived in Ephesus and encountered a group of "disciples." He immediately noticed, however, that something essential was lacking. He inquired whether they had received the Holy Spirit when they came to believe, and they informed him that they had never even heard of the Holy Spirit. With that information, Paul did not preach about receiving a second blessing of the Holy Spirit but instead shared the story of Jesus. And when they believed and were baptized, he laid hands on them, and they were filled with the Holy Spirit.

I often wonder if Paul were to visit our Christian endeavors today, would he immediately recognize something missing? We often make church nothing more than an event emphasizing what *we* can *do*, with or without the Holy Spirit. Our personalities, talents, programs, and buildings are usually far more noticeable than the fruit of the Spirit (Galatians 5:22–23). Christians have a reputation in this world for many things other than love, joy, peace, and faithfulness. A.W. Tozer once quipped: "If the Holy Spirit was withdrawn from the church today, 95 percent of what we do would go on and no one would know the difference. If the Holy Spirit had been withdrawn from the New Testament church, 95 percent of what they did would stop, and everybody would know the difference."

The title of Luke's second volume in our Bibles (the first being the Gospel of Luke) is the *Acts of the Apostles*—but really it should be called the *Acts of the Holy Spirit*. I've counted 57 times in the 28 chapters of Acts that the Holy Spirit is referred to in some manner.

In the book of Acts, the Holy Spirit is immediately noticeable. His presence is noticed on the first day (Acts 2:5–13). Even the enemies of the disciples notice the Spirit of Jesus in them (Acts 4:13). Leaders at that time were chosen not for their doctrinal correctness, level of education, or prowess in preaching. In stark contrast to how it is usually done today, leaders were selected on how recognizable the Holy Spirit was in their lives (Acts 6:3). It is remarkable that salvation for the Gentiles (thus opening a door to a whole new view of what it meant to be saved) was verified by the immediate presence of the Holy Spirit (Acts 11:15–18). This was the evidence that was weighed and found sufficient rather than circumcision, and that changed everything. I often wonder what would change in the world if the fruit of the Holy Spirit—love, joy, peace, patience, kindness, goodness, faithfulness, gentleness, and self-control—was what followers of Jesus were most known for.

Equally significant were those times when the Holy Spirit was *not* evident, such as among the Samaritans before Peter and John laid hands on them (Acts 8:14–24). And now, in Ephesus. Paul immediately recognized that something was wrong (Acts 19:1–7).

Frankly, having the Spirit of the eternal God, holy and all-powerful, take up residence in your body should be noticeable, not just to you, but to everyone around you (1 Corinthians 6:18-19; Colossians 1:27b). To our shame, I am not sure that we are able to recognize the presence or absence of the Holy Spirit as readily as they did in the New Testament. In fact, all surveys for the past few decades reveal that there is little difference in lifestyle between those who claim to be Christians and those who do not. The rates of divorce, addiction, greed, jealousy, and gossip are essentially equal for both Christians and non-Christians.

It was not the spiritual gifts, whether of tongues or something else, that really made a Spirit-filled church recognizable. The Corinthian church had every gift (1 Corinthians 1:7) but was carnal and full of divisions and even the sort of immorality that made the pagans blush (1 Corinthians 3:2-4, 5:1–2). The *gifts* of the Spirit are not as important as the *fruit* of the Spirit. Jesus told us that we would recognize people of good or bad influence by the fruit in their lives. Some people with miraculous gifts used in the name of the Lord didn't even know him (Matthew 7:15-23). People can use their spiritual gifts in a selfish manner, but they cannot exhibit love in a selfish way. Wherever spiritual gifts are talked about in the New Testament, love is mentioned in a very conspicuous manner (Romans 12:9-10; 1 Corinthians 13:1-13; Ephesians 4:2, 15-16; 1 Peter 4:8). This is by divine design.

Is love the most noticeable thing in our churches? Is that what people pick up on immediately when they join us? We need more of the Spirit and less of ourselves in the way we function as the people of God. Spiritual gifts are wonderful, but the greatest gift is love (1 Corinthians 12:31–13:13). Even though the first apostles are gone, I believe we can still experience the *Acts of the Holy Spirit*, and I will remain hopeful and vigilant as we all write Acts 29 and following.

Paul Establishes a Beachhead in Ephesus

As was his pattern, Paul arrived in Ephesus and immediately began to teach in the synagogue. He did this for three months until the Jews finally began to oppose him, and then he withdrew. He then found another place to meet where he could share the gospel in public—the school of Tyrannus.

We do not know much about the man Tyrannus, but his name is mentioned in the archaeological finds of Ephesus, and so his actual existence is verified in extrabiblical sources.[2] Judging from the language used to describe Paul's work there, "school" (*skolai*) was the place where philosophers taught; and "reasoning" (*dialegomai*) was how philosophers engaged with their students.[3] It is therefore safe to assume that Tyrannus was a philosophical teacher who had a school that rented space to Paul. The Western text (an ancient manuscript on which the King James Bible translation is based) includes an additional line that says that Paul would meet there and teach from eleven in the morning until four in the afternoon.

This is quite plausible, given that midday hours are when most of the people in the city would have rested to escape the hot sun. Some sources say that more Ephesians would have been awake at one o'clock in the morning than at one in the afternoon.[4] Paul may have made tents in the morning hours as well as later in the afternoon (Acts 20:35). Then, while most of the city was resting, he would have done the exhausting work of training the new disciples. He followed this pattern for two full years.[5]

This. Is. War.

Ephesus, situated where the Cayster River met the Aegean Sea, was a center for commercial enterprise and had a population of 51,000 people. Although it competed with Pergamum (the political capital) for influence, there is no doubt that, culturally and commercially, it was the leading city of the region. One of the seven wonders of the ancient world was in this highly influential city—the temple of Artemis. This gigantic temple, with 127 columns, stood 60 feet tall and was 425 feet long and 220 feet wide. With a footprint much larger than an American football field, it dwarfed all other structures in the city, both physically and culturally.[6]

Ephesus was world famous for this temple and for the worship of Artemis, a Greek goddess of the hunt, wild animals, wilderness, fertility, childbirth, virginity, and young girls; she was reported to both bring and relieve disease in women. Many people there believed that the statue of Artemis (a multi-breasted female goddess) found in the temple had simply fallen from the sky and that Ephesus was its guardian.

With this belief in Artemis as a spiritual foundation of sorts, the people of the city were captivated by superstition. The temple was not only a commercial enterprise but also created a spiritual identity that held the hearts and minds of the people in bondage to fear and false beliefs. Magic, including spells and charms, was a big part of the culture of Ephesus. In this dark environment, Paul set out to instigate a spiritual uprising throughout Asia Minor that would overthrow evil and establish a work that could not be stopped.

Paul knew that we cannot simply enter a place and see the world as only material with merely human influences at work. All that we see, feel, taste, touch, and hear is only a portion of what is real. There is an unsensed, spiritual world that is just as real and that influences our lives profoundly, although we are often blind to it. In fact, it has greater impact on what governs our lives than the material world around us (2 Corinthians 4:4; Ephesians 2:1-2; 1 John 5:19; Revelation 12:9). We see governments, businesses, and culture, but we do not see the ancient spiritual influences beneath all these established human institutions. They are indeed there, and their influences are real and evil.

Ignoring these unperceived spiritual realities will seriously hamper our attempts to produce significant results in either world. To truly transform a culture, it is not enough to just start multiple Christian gatherings. The gospel must make inroads into all of society. Our influence should go beyond the seats and hit the streets. Our efforts on behalf of God's Kingdom are to be effective in both the material and the spiritual world. To do that we must focus our powerful work in both the seen and the unseen realms.

Christ stands alone. You cannot simply add Jesus to the many other gods worshipped in a city. He is the one true God and rules over all false gods and demonic entities that lay claim on a people. Jesus is countercultural, so when His Kingdom truly comes to a place, human institutions get turned upside down because the King of kings invades and rules the hearts, minds, and actions of His people.

That was the case at Ephesus. The gospel overturned the dark strongholds of this city and set people free from their bondage to the occult. Paul saw wondrous miracles occur in Ephesus that revealed to everyone that there was indeed a more powerful way of living.

The Ephesians who held positions of influence and who profited from the worship of Artemis understood that Paul's message was a direct threat to their way of life. They commented, "Not only is there danger that this trade of ours fall into disrepute, but also that the temple of the great goddess Artemis be regarded as worthless and that she whom all of Asia and the world worship will even be dethroned from her magnificence" (Acts 19:27). They understood. Those on both sides of the battlelines knew that this was an all-out war, spiritual in nature, and the spoils would go to the victor. There would indeed be a winner and a loser. Those who had a vested interest in the old system understood that this was a spiritual fight for the soul of Asia Minor. Often, those in a place who are deeply involved in the strongholds of evil are acutely aware of the threat that the Kingdom of God brings—sadly, much more aware than those in the Church.

We must see the cities of this world with spiritual eyes and not just physical ones. We need bigger goals worthy of Jesus. Increasing the number of people sitting in an event between 10:00 AM and noon one day a week will never bring this kind of radical change to a place. Don't be satisfied with anything less than the transformation Christ and His Kingdom are fully capable of.

Today there is hardly anything left of the cult of Artemis worship as it existed in Paul's day in that place. The great temple was destroyed, then rebuilt and destroyed again. Today there is nothing left of this grand edifice except for a single reconstructed column that remains in a muddy field. The letter that Paul wrote to the Ephesian church, however, is still as powerful in changing lives as when it was first written.

When Paul later wrote to the Ephesians, he reminded them that it had been a spiritual war: "For our struggle is not against flesh and blood, but against the rulers, against the powers, against the world forces of this darkness, against the spiritual forces of wickedness in the heavenly places" (Ephesians 6:12). These words reminded them of the reality they experienced in this spiritual battle initiated by Paul's coming. The Bible clearly teaches us that we have an adversary, a spiritual being that rules over the demonic world that we do not see. Paul calls this being "the prince of the power of the air" (Ephesians 2:2). It may feel as if Satan is everywhere at once and all-knowing, but only Almighty God is. Nevertheless, Satan does have an army of fallen angels and demonic entities at his command that are deployed in all the cities and places where people live.

In fact, all our cities and nations are under his rule. When Jesus was tempted by the devil, "… he led Him up and showed Him all the kingdoms of the world in a moment of time. And the devil said to Him, 'I will give You *all this domain* and its glory; for it has been *handed over to me*, and I give it to whomever I wish. Therefore if You worship before me, it shall all be Yours.' Jesus answered him, 'It is written, "You shall worship the Lord your God and serve Him only."'" (Luke 4:5-8, emphasis added).

The devil is still at work and still claims the kingdoms of this world.

Paul faced that same evil in Asia Minor. We are foolish to think that our nations, cities, and towns are spiritually neutral and that humans and their ideas are our only obstacle to expanding Christ's Kingdom. Our true influence must actively oppose the powers that rule over this world (1 John 5:19).

When Paul entered Asia Minor to expand the reign of Christ by setting spiritual captives free from this demonic rule, he entered into perhaps the most hostile spiritual environment in the world at that time. When Jesus, in the book of Revelation, spoke to the seven churches that were begun during Paul's third journey in this very region, He acknowledged some spiritual influences in the region that we need to take note of. Seventy-five miles north of Ephesus was the capital city of Pergamum. Jesus, in His message to the Pergamum church, boldly stated that the throne of Satan was there (Revelation 2:13), and many people speculate that this may refer to the grand altar built to Zeus that sat atop the highly fortified acropolis of Pergamum.[7] This city was the political seat of authority over Asia Minor. The creatures of the demonic realm recognize and often even draw geographical boundaries based upon authority they have usurped.

This new work Paul began in Ephesus faced extremely harsh spiritual conflicts. Perhaps that offers a clue to why the Lord forbade Paul to speak the gospel in Asia Minor before he had learned the lessons of his second journey. This delay was not only about strategy that had to be learned but also about character fortification and increasing spiritual authority in Paul's life. On his second journey, he was not yet ready to face the ruler of all demons, fallen angels, and the world (1 John 5:19; Revelation 12:9).

In Ephesus, a place full of superstition and longing for spiritual power, Paul showed up. Through his hands many sick people were healed, and demonic spirits were cast out as people were set free by the gospel. Even articles of clothing taken from Paul healed and released people from demonic bondage (Acts 19:11). This must have powerfully impressed a crowd that was accustomed to the magic arts.

But there were still other cultural and spiritual aspects to consider. In that culture, there was also a strong combination of fear and jealousy. In such a spiritually dark and superstitious environment, Jewish magicians were somehow also considered especially powerful. Because the Jews would not pronounce the name of God so as to avoid using it in vain and to keep the third of the Ten Commandments (Exodus 20:7), much of the Gentile world believed God's name carried extremely potent magic. In Luke's narrative of Acts, he records three encounters with Jewish magicians: the first was with Simon in Samaria (Acts 8:9–13); the second, with Elymas in Cyprus (Acts 13:6–12); and the third here in Ephesus—most notably with a group of brothers. In Acts 19:13–20, Luke tells us about "Jewish exorcists who went from place to place" and mentions the seven sons of Sceva.

These men, when they cast spells, tried to invoke what they saw as Paul's magic by using the same words Paul had used. But one time when Sceva's sons tried that in exorcising an evil spirit, they discovered that Paul's words were not a magic incantation but a true reflection of something much greater, based on real spiritual authority, which they did not possess. The demon acknowledged Jesus and Paul but then proceeded to beat and humiliate the seven brothers. In contrast, Paul's own spiritual authority was growing by the day. As people were released from captivity, they were immediately trained and deployed in God's service. When they believed in Christ and abandoned sorcery, they soon realized that this new faith was far more powerful than any magic.

These true conversions became known throughout Ephesus when the new Christians collected all the magic parchments they owned and burned them in a massive bonfire. They declared boldly and publicly that they would no longer remain enslaved to magic spells, curses, and charms.[8] It was not an option for the Ephesians to simply add Jesus to their current cultural and religious mindset. The gospel of Christ demanded an all-or-nothing surrender to Jesus as King, and the new believers demonstrated this with their actions. We are required to take up our own cross and follow Him as the first step in our spiritual walk; anything less results in an anemic church that claims Christianity but shows none of the real thing. Once we have surrendered our life (which is what carrying a cross alludes to), it is easy to surrender our false gods and the devices of our former spiritual practices, even if doing so represents a great amount of money. In this case, it was equivalent to fifty thousand pieces of silver. This was more than a public display. It was a public change of allegiance in a spiritual conflict for the souls of people. It was war. Luke says, "So the word of the Lord was growing mightily and *prevailing*" (Acts 19:20, emphasis mine).

The Ephesians who made their living by making and selling the paraphernalia of superstition soon saw that this turn of events was bad for business and bad for the worship of Artemis, so they instigated a riot, causing great confusion in the city. Many people rushed into the large theater, chanting, "Great is Artemis of the Ephesians!" Try to imagine an outdoor stadium full of twenty-five thousand people all shouting with one voice, "Great is Artemis of the Ephesians!" (I even imagine seeing a beach ball or two being bounced around, with an occasional "wave" initiated and someone selling peanuts, but my imagination can be a bit excessive.) Eventually, level heads prevailed, and the assembly of angry people disbanded and returned to their homes.[9]

Shortly after this mob dispersed and every soul in all of Asia Minor had heard the message of Christ, Paul went off to Macedonia and Greece to visit the churches from the previous journey and then move on to Jerusalem to bring funds for relief of the famine there. After that mission was accomplished, his intent was to go to the capital of the world—Rome.

Incredible Fruitfulness

This third missionary journey is set apart from the others by its amazing effectiveness. It is one thing to see the incredible results that occurred in the city of Ephesus, but that was just the beginning. New churches were started all across Asia Minor during these three years. The good news of Jesus was heard by every person in the entire region.

The seven churches of Asia Minor mentioned in the opening chapters of Revelation were some of the results from this journey where the apostle stayed in one place. During these three years, churches were started not just in Ephesus but also in Smyrna, Pergamum, Thyatira, Sardis, Philadelphia, and Laodicea. The churches in Colossae and Hierapolis also owe their beginnings to this missionary journey.

Although Paul wrote the apostolic letter to the Colossian church, he did not plant it. In fact, he mentions that the Colossians have never even seen his face (Colossians 2:1). If Paul didn't start this church that he wrote to, who did? A man named Epaphras is likely the one who began the

Colossian church (Colossians 1:6–8) as well as the ones in Hierapolis and Laodicea. Epaphras was Paul's disciple and was originally from the area of these three cities (Colossians 4:11–13), which are all in the region called the Lycus River Valley. He likely came to know Christ in Ephesus, received some effective mentoring there, and then returned to his homeland armed with the gospel and a new apostolic call. He was so good at following in his mentor's footsteps that we eventually find him in jail beside Paul (Philemon 23).

Paul is considered the apostolic leader and the grandfather of all these churches. He referred to himself as "Paul, the aged" to Philemon, who hosted a church in his home in Colossae (Philemon 9). Although it was Epaphras who began the work, Paul also mentioned that Philemon owed his own life to Paul (Philemon 19), even though the two may not have met. Paul understood how to extend his apostolic foundation without needing to be physically present. He learned to work through others rather than doing everything by himself. He discovered this principle of multiplication in the depths of the second journey, but he perfected it on the third.

Epaphras was just one of many disciples that Paul trained and sent throughout Asia Minor. It was such a far-reaching work that Luke recounts the success of this journey by stating emphatically that every single person who lived in Asia heard the message of God, whether Jew or Gentile (Acts 19:10). That is incredible. Even Paul's enemies said of him during this time, "You see and hear that not only in Ephesus, but in almost all of Asia, this Paul has persuaded and turned away a considerable number of people, saying that gods made with hands are no gods at all" (Acts 19:26).

The Inevitable Cost

The powerful breakthroughs Paul saw in such dark places as Ephesus and Asia Minor came at a high cost. Luke mentions little of the trials Paul endured on this journey, but there are still glimpses of them found in the New Testament.

While reporting on this fruitful work to the Corinthians, Paul mentions that he faced some strong opposition (1 Corinthians 16:9). We might assume that he is referring to the incident with the mob at the theater, but I believe there was much more that Paul endured. He mentions to the elders of the Ephesian churches that he did not shrink back when facing trials brought about by the plots of the Jews during these three years (Acts 20:19), which certainly is not the riot instigated by the Artemis worshippers. Not all of his opposition is reported in Acts. He even mentions having to fight off wild beasts in Ephesus (1 Corinthians 15:32). That conjures up all kinds of possible scenarios. Perhaps he is alluding to a Roman form of entertainment in which prisoners were forced to face wild animals in the stadium to fight for their freedom. But there are other possible explanations. As I mentioned, Artemis of the Ephesians was a goddess of wild beasts, so this may reflect a specific demonic attack utilizing wild animals that Paul faced while attempting to break the hold this fallen angel had over the Ephesians. The spiritual conflict between the Kingdom of God and the dark rulership of Satan can manifest in many ways. A demonic ruler of wild beasts could have sent some Paul's way. The burdens Paul had to face while working in Ephesus were so heavy that at one point he lost all his strength and even despaired of life itself (2 Corinthians 1:8–11).

Taking on the throne of Satan and all the spiritual forces in that region took its toll on the apostle. If he hadn't been prepared for this through the important spiritual formation and strategic lessons learned on the second journey, he might not have made it through the third. This, I believe, is the best reason why Paul was forbidden to preach the gospel in Asia Minor during his second journey. He needed the depth of character, discernment, understanding, spiritual authority, and principles of reproductive ministry he learned on that journey to enable him to leave this one alive. Remember that when Paul arrived in Corinth on his second journey, he was full of fear. If he had come to Ephesus in that condition he would have been devoured.

This third journey was a study in contrasts. It was easy and it was hard at the same time. Paul's gifts, calling, skills, strategy, spiritual formation, and deep character all came together in a work that spread with incredible speed and power. This is evident convergence in a spiritual life. At the same time, the opposition was so extreme that it nearly killed Paul more than once.

Most people serving God today find the two contrasting things sadly reversed. The work is hard, and it costs much money, sweat, and tears to get measly results. The spiritual opposition, however, is weak and unimpressive. It is almost as if the enemy is fine with what we are currently doing and doesn't want it to stop. In contrast to our experience in Western Christianity, if you talk with church leaders doing work in rapidly multiplying Jesus movements (such as in China or Iran) they will tell you that the ministry is easy and spreads quickly, but that the persecution, spiritual warfare, and tests of character are magnified exponentially.

Perhaps if we gained the spiritual strength Paul developed over the course of his journeys, we too might face tougher opposition and see greater impact on the world with efforts that bear fruit well beyond expectation. G. K. Chesterton once wrote in his book *What's Wrong with the World*, "The Christian ideal has not been tried and found wanting. It has been found difficult; and left untried."

After Asia

After Ephesus, Paul went to Macedonia and Greece. There is some evidence that when he went to Macedonia, he took the Egnatian Way west and then ventured up into Illyricum (modern Albania). We can conclude this because he mentioned in his letter to the Romans, written at the end of the third journey, that he had preached the gospel as far as Illyricum (Romans 15:19). He does not appear to have ventured that far northwest on any previous journey, and this is the only gap in this journey where such a trip seems plausible prior to the composition of that Roman letter. It appears that Paul had learned his new strategy well but was still an apostle who "aspired to preach the gospel, not where Christ was already named, so that I would not build on another man's foundation" (Romans 15:20).

Still later on this third journey, Paul is seen traveling with a band that was larger than ever before (Acts 20:4-5). In fact, the members seem to represent all his missional efforts, and for good reasons. Luke mentions Sopater of Berea, Aristarchus and Secundus of Thessalonica, Gaius and Timothy of Derbe/Lystra, Tychicus and Trophimus of Asia, and Luke. There is a strong possibility, based on other epistles, that Titus was also with the group (2 Corinthians 8:6–23, 12:18).

The best explanation of why so many men were traveling with Paul is that he was collecting funds from all the Gentile churches to distribute in Jerusalem for famine relief (1 Corinthians 16:3). Therefore, there were two very good reasons for such a delegation—first, to have representation from all the churches when the gift was delivered, and second, to discourage robbers from stealing what they had collected, which was a common challenge Paul faced (2 Corinthians 11:26).

Your Story: Lessons of the Third Journey

In a masterful stroke, Luke anticipated that we would wonder how Paul could have been so extremely fruitful in such a short time. He tells us the answer without veering from the narrative style of the book of Acts. In chapter 20, Luke presents us with more information about this missionary journey by recording Paul's explanation to the elders of the Ephesian church of how he had done his work. After his farewell address to them on the beach in Miletus, Paul and his companions continue their journey to Jerusalem. If we analyze the short message Paul gives on the beach, we can discover some clues as to how he was so effective on this journey.

Selection of a Strategic Base to Reach an Entire Region

Paul established a regional base of spiritual formation in Ephesus, a world-class city that had significant trade passing through its streets (Acts 19:9). With an estimated population of 51,000, Ephesus was the true city of cultural and commercial influence in Asia Minor. Pergamum may have been the political capital of the region, but Ephesus was the heart. It is not a stretch to believe that if Paul were choosing where to set up a base today, he would pick Istanbul over Ankara, and New York City over Washington, D.C.; with this strategy, ultimately, he would get Ankara and Washington as well.

Jesus instructed the Twelve (Matthew 10:11-12) and the Seventy (Luke 10:5-7) disciples to find a person of peace and stay in that place as they impacted that community. He even commanded them to not go from door to door. To those he trained in Ephesus, Paul was able to say, "You yourselves know, from the first day I set foot in Asia, how I was with you the whole time" (Acts 20:18). Paul had to learn this lesson on his second journey, and with Jesus' powerful message to him in Corinth, he did. He applied the lesson well as he stayed in Ephesus for three years, and all who lived in Asia Minor heard the message of Jesus.

Increased Spiritual and Relational Authority

As we have seen, Paul had exceptional spiritual authority that allowed him to take on the highest levels of demonic beings and live to tell about it. That spiritual authority was not only reserved for spirit beings but also evident in the way he interacted with flesh and blood people.

The personal attacks and trials Paul endured conferred authority on his life. His scars were a calling card for his apostleship, and those who followed Jesus respected him because of them. He would often point to those scars and experiences as the true evidence that he was indeed an apostle (2 Corinthians 4:8–12, 11:21–29; Galatians 6:17). The way he faced his trials, without shrinking from the cost of doing the work, showed the Ephesian elders that he was a man willing to pay the price many times over for what he believed (Acts 20:19–20).

Paul gave the Holy Spirit His rightful place in leading disciples into ministry. He said, "Be on guard for yourselves and for all the flock, among which the Holy Spirit has made you overseers" (Acts 20:28). Paul had learned to train the leaders to rely on the Holy Spirit rather than on him.

On his first journey, he and Barnabas appointed elders from among the new believers (Acts 14:23), but after two additional journeys, Paul had a more mature outlook. Realizing that the responsibility for raising elders rested with the One who will always be there for those leaders, he pointedly reminds them that it was not he but the Holy Spirit who appointed them to lead. In a sense, Paul had no intention of returning to visit Ephesus several times, as he had needed to do with the Galatian churches (Acts 20:25). In fact, he went out of his way to avoid visiting Ephesus on his return trip; instead, Paul landed in Miletus and asked the Ephesian elders to come to him (Acts 20:16), where he informed them that they would likely never see him again.

This may seem like merely a semantic argument, especially given Paul's later instructions to Titus to appoint elders (Titus 1:5). When Paul was instructing Titus to appoint elders in every city of Crete, it was being done in a pioneering church planting work. In other words, he is instructing Titus to commission church planting leaders to go about the island to start new works. This is indeed similar to what Paul did in Ephesus. Paul would identify those that the Holy Spirit was raising up and mentor them (such as Epaphras); when they were ready, he sent them to the cities all over Asia Minor. I believe that is what he is instructing Titus to do as well.

I believe that the concept of raising leaders who were less dependent on their mentor and more dependent on the sufficiency of the Holy Spirit is indeed a profound lesson Paul learned since his first journey, and one that bore significant fruit this time around. As a result of this lesson, the churches started on the third journey were far more self-sufficient than those started on the first trip.

Although the Ephesian church's beginning was marked by the absence of the Holy Spirit (Acts 19:1-7), that was quickly corrected. The Holy Spirit's presence would soon mean everything in the life of this church and all the other churches she would birth. Paul told the Ephesian elders that even though they might not see his face again, the Holy Spirit would always be present (Acts 20:32). This is a good reminder to us all. Here again we see the convergence of Paul's experiences and growth in personal spiritual maturity as he encourages the Ephesians to be utterly dependent on the Holy Spirit.

Doing the Work While Doing Life

Paul's authority was also based on his example of integrity. His words matched his actions, which is always characteristic of true authority. Paul labored among the people at his own trade of making tents. Some people have questioned whether Paul's vocational work was helpful or hurtful to his missionary efforts. They point out that the places where he spent relatively little time (such as Philippi and Thessalonica) had what appear to have been healthier churches, while the places where he stayed and worked at his trade (such as Corinth) had churches that were not as healthy. I have a different perspective.

In the first place, I've already pointed out that while Paul left Philippi and Thessalonica after staying only a short time, he also left behind in each of these places a mentor (Luke and Timothy, respectively) to help train the emerging church. The Galatian churches were started quickly but then left without any mentoring support. It seems that these first-journey churches were the weakest of his church plants and required more personal visits and sterner letters than any others.[10]

The Corinthian church's troubles required at least three letters from Paul, written to address some very serious problems.[11] It is true that Paul worked his trade there, but when Timothy and Silas rejoined him, he stopped making tents and started giving all his time to ministry. Some churches he previously started probably provided some financial support (2 Corinthians 11:8), and his coworkers earned enough income to free him up to serve (Acts 18:5; 2 Corinthians 11:9). It appears that almost the opposite occurred in Ephesus, where Paul says he worked with his own hands the entire time to support even those who were on his apostolic team (Acts 20:34). This was a reversal of what occurred in Corinth. I believe that this was an important shift for Paul—another key lesson learned and applied. The problems found in the Corinthian church certainly reflected the severe temptations associated with its unique location. If anything, however, there is evidence that Paul made tents there only for a short time and then poured himself full time into the church work. Perhaps through trial and error, he realized the shortcomings of that strategy as well, so that when he went to Ephesus, he did the opposite. Those who disparage "tent making" would not claim that the Ephesian church was less healthy than even the Philippian or Thessalonian churches. I believe that the letters written to those churches had several purposes, including correcting very specific problems, but the letter to the Ephesian church was broader in scope. It was likely meant to be circulated to encourage all churches universally, and there is not a single person or problem that he specifically corrected in the letter.

The establishment of the Ephesian church was remarkable in that it ultimately saturated an entire population with churches using common people as change agents. These people more than likely came into contact with Paul through their trades and probably continued in their work as they took Jesus with them to their hometowns and beyond. By working as he did, Paul established a life pattern that they could all follow, and he set the tone for an all-volunteer movement. He led by example, weaving spirituality and service to Christ into his everyday activities. Many disciples followed this example, and an entire population heard the good news of Jesus.

Even though they spend less time working in a trade, missionaries and other full-time workers who are fully supported financially are not automatically more efficient or effective. Paul demonstrated that doing his job as a full-time tentmaker while also training indigenous leaders could work incredibly well. Perhaps the very things we think will make us more efficient actually keep us from achieving the effectiveness we long to see. Paul serves as a model of someone whose work for God was helped and not hindered by the ebb and flow of real life. Paul was able to ask more of those he trained, and they rose to the challenge, following his personal example. He also established a mission work that was not dependent on the missionary, because it was not done by a fully supported professional. In this way, he did not set the bar so high that none of the indigenous leaders could emulate him.

Here again, Paul finds himself following the specific teachings of Jesus regarding the mission. In the sermon of Jesus to the Seventy recorded in Luke's Gospel, he says, "Carry no money belt" (Luke 10:4). He instructs the apostolic teams to not go with financial backing. This is so that those they reach will feel able to imitate the practice and the gospel of the Kingdom can spread indigenously from household to household, village to village, city to city, and nation to nation.

Paul points back to his own hard work as a source of authority that comes by example so that others will follow. He says, "You yourselves know that these hands ministered to my own needs and to the men who were with me. In everything I showed you that by working hard in this manner you must help the weak and remember the words of the Lord Jesus, that He Himself said, 'It is more blessed to give than to receive'" (Acts 20:34–35). His hard work is also evidence that he was not serving out of questionable motives (Acts 20:33)—a demonstration that I believe is needed today.

Years of following Christ through the journeys of life will produce insight that cannot be faked or bought. We see a small glimpse of Paul's perspective, gained from decades of experience, when he confidently replies to the elders, "I know that after my departure savage wolves will come in among you, not sparing the flock; and from among your own selves men will arise, speaking perverse things, to draw away the disciples after them" (Acts 20:29–30). These are not simply prophetic words. There are scars and many tears underlying them.

Strategic, Experiential, and Holistic Training

Paul constantly mentored individuals on a one-to-one basis. He said, "… night and day for a period of three years I did not cease to admonish *each one* with tears" (Acts 20:31, emphasis added). He seemed to hold back nothing from his apprentices. Paul integrated learning both in public venues such as the school of Tyrannus and in the settings where life normally took place, following the natural paths of life from household (*oikos*) to household (Acts 20:19–20). The spiritual formation of Paul's disciples had evangelism as a foundation for training in ministry (Acts 20:21). His apprentices learned truth not just by studying or memorizing God's Word but especially by obeying it and speaking it boldly. Nothing cements the truth of the gospel in our own life like giving it away to others and defending it from critics as we do.

Here is a summary of the ways Paul trained his apprentices:

a. Through daily public dialogue in the school of Tyrannus as well as working out that training in their home life along the paths of natural relationships (Acts 20:20).
b. With personal and vulnerable one-on-one mentoring (Acts 20:31).
c. And by example with literal on-the-job training (Acts 20:33–35).

There is not just one way to train people. Everyone is unique and learns in a variety of ways. If we always use one unvarying method to train our potential disciples, we will only reach a fraction of the available people, and we will likely only touch a small portion of their lives. We can truly know them and bring out the best in each of them by working with them one-on-one in the ebb and flow of real life. Paul knew his disciples well, and they also knew him deeply. There is a place and time for more public dialogue with those you train, like the school of Tyrannus. If that is your only venue for training, however, you will never see the kind of impactful results Paul saw in his three years in Ephesus. You must also mentor one-on-one and be open and vulnerable as you do. You need to take the students out into the world and have them live out their faith where life happens. This is how we multiply workers for the Kingdom.

Paul learned these concepts on previous journeys but solidified them and made significant advances while in Ephesus. The results were astounding. We must be holistic in our approach to training those who would carry Christ to the world.

Raising Up and Sending Out Leaders in a Short Time Frame

As demonstrated above, Paul developed indigenous leaders in such a way that they could carry on the work without needing his presence. They were deployed in service immediately. They were focused primarily on Christ from the first day they believed. They were trained in their faith with immediate obedience to preach the gospel to others (Acts 20:21).

Paul held nothing back from his disciples: he wept with them (Acts 20:31), communicated to each the entire purpose of God (Acts 20:27), and warned them of coming hostilities (Acts 20:29). He even foretold some of their own future betrayals (Acts 20:30). Paul released the power of God's Word in people's lives to carry forward the grassroots movement of multiplication (Acts 19:20).

As we have discussed, some believe that the initiator of a work should leave a place quickly instead of remaining there to teach and lead, hoping that this will make the new leaders who have been raised up more independent. That is not the case. This has been tried with missionaries in cross-cultural settings and even with church-planting efforts in same culture situations. I am not arguing for lifelong service in one place. I do not believe that anyone who actually has an apostolic gifting could do that anyway. But I am finding that if a church is started and the missionary leaves before emerging disciples can be mentored and trained, the church members often feel abandoned and inadequate. This situation fuels a desire for more dependency, not less. Jesus stayed with his band of leaders three years, and that is also how long Paul stayed in Ephesus. Perhaps we should look longer at this length of time for pioneer missionary enterprise as well as church starting initiatives. Is it possible that Paul, having stayed a year and a half in Corinth, left when his work was only half done? Perhaps there would have been less problems in the church if he had stayed twice as long. This is pure conjecture, but it's a thought worth considering.

It is important to clarify that Paul remained in Ephesus three years and after that period every person in Asia Minor had heard the gospel. That doesn't mean that he took three years to train each disciple and *then* sent them out. It means that he trained them in a much shorter period and sent them out so that in those three years the entire region was fully saturated with Jesus' message. In today's church world being a believer for less than three years usually means that the disciple is immature and not ready to be sent. That is not how Jesus did His work, and it is obviously not how Paul did as well.

Did Paul have an exit strategy even before he had an entrance strategy for Asia Minor? It certainly appears that his stay for three years was planned (Acts 20:31). He empowered his leaders with accountability to God for the work that he modeled for them, and so his presence wasn't needed for the work to continue when he left (Acts 20:32).

Paul did not merely give theory for the emerging leaders to learn after he departed. It was proved to them throughout the three years as Paul trained and sent apostolic missionaries and workers out all over the region. They knew that what Paul had prepared them for was possible. They wept at the good-bye, not because they felt inadequate to the task but simply because they loved Paul and would likely not see him again this side of heaven (Acts 20:36–38).

People who, like Paul, have made it through the years of lonely character development, humbling failures, and faith-building successes can rightly be called third-journey leaders, even as they acknowledge their utter dependence on the Lord. What are some of their qualities? The maturity and wisdom earned from third-journey leaders' life experiences are easy to spot. These men and women have a confidence and a perspective that is both attractive (drawing in) and empowering (sending out) at the same time. They are trusted because they are trust*worthy*. Because of these attributes, third-journey leaders tend to attract more apprentices, and those apprentices are more serious about the mentoring process.

These younger (in either age or maturity) followers do not feel like they are being used for their mentor's projects—actually, quite the opposite. They feel that their success is of more value to their mentor than his own reputation. Why? Because it truly is. Third-journey leaders have proved that they are good stewards of God's valuable assets, and that is why God trusts them with His greatest resources—passionate women and men who will take the gospel further than their mentors ever could. The message of a third-journey person expands and multiplies through the voices and lives of others. The apprentices take the third-journey person's work and writings further than their mentor ever dreamed possible.

Doing More by Doing Less

Third-journey leaders are continuing to learn the secret of accomplishing more while doing less. At this stage multiplication kicks up the effectiveness thirtyfold, sixtyfold, or a hundredfold (Matthew 13:23). This journey, while not lacking in hard work and difficult trials, often sees production well beyond the previous ratio of result to effort. The amount of well-focused effort seems to multiply its fruitfulness exponentially on a third journey. The work of the third journey grows much farther geographically because others carry the work where we couldn't go ourselves. Where one person can only go on one path at a time, five workers can go in five different directions simultaneously. This is how a third-journey person sees his or her efforts expand exponentially.

Third-journey people know that their time is limited and work in such a way that they are not needed afterward. They see themselves as disposable, which in fact makes them some of the most valuable people in God's Kingdom. When they move on, the work continues and even thrives in their absence.

Third-Journey Reflections

So now is the time for self-evaluation. If you aspire to be like Paul in the third-journey season, ask yourself the following reflection questions.

- Have you reproduced Christ in others? If you were removed from your own ministry service, what would remain? Are the people you trained leaving their old ways, taking up the cross, and taking Jesus to other people and places?
- Are you more concerned for the success of the people you have mentored than for your own success?
- Are you finding that you have hard won experience that provides answers and powerful solutions to whatever challenges you face? Do you face more severe spiritual resistance from the enemy than you ever did before? Is your confrontation with evil obvious, and are you dramatically victorious?
- Do your efforts seem small compared to the great results you are seeing birthed by them? Are you amazed at the high quality and growing number of people who are joining your work? Does the work seem easier, carried on the shoulders of many people, but the attacks from the enemy more intense? Are you humbled that such high-quality people respond to your invitations to join you?

If these questions are a challenge for you, then perhaps you are still working your way through an earlier journey. I would estimate that most leaders in the West are still at the level of their first or second journey. If more people were on the third journey, I believe we would see far more reproduction of disciples, leaders, and churches, as well as a greater impact on society and culture. Our enemy would be far more concerned with what we are doing and resist forcefully with all his strength. Hopefully these times are still ahead for us. If, like most people, you don't find yourself in this phase of maturity yet, don't be discouraged. Let this chapter serve as an incentive that gives you something worth looking forward to as you press through the earlier journeys.

Those few who have blossomed into their third journey have come to experience a whole new level of fruitfulness and convergence. As hard to imagine as it is, there is still one more journey that can bring the *most* impact on the world. As we will see in the next chapter, Paul's fourth journey was his most significant in many ways.

CHAPTER 6

THE FOURTH JOURNEY
All Roads Lead to Rome

Success is not to be pursued; it is to be attracted by the person you become.
—Jim Rohn

Now I want you to know, brethren, that my circumstances have turned out for the greater progress of the gospel.
—Paul describing his fourth journey (Philippians 1:12)

We do not usually consider Paul's various imprisonments by the Roman authorities as a missionary journey, but I assure you, Paul did. He had intended to go to Rome (Romans 1:14–16), and on this trip the Roman Empire covered the cost of getting there. What is surprising is that Paul considered this to be his most effective missionary journey, even though he spent most of the time incarcerated.

When Paul wrote to the Philippians while under house arrest in Rome, he explained that those circumstances were enabling him to be more effective in proclaiming the gospel around the world than when he had been free to travel (Philippians 1:12). Let the significance of this statement sink in a bit. Paul was saying that being in prison was actually allowing him to have a greater global impact than he had been able to have when he could travel and preach the gospel wherever he wanted. How was that possible?

The impact of Paul's previous journeys had been regional, for the most part, either when he was starting churches in particular cities or spreading the gospel over an entire area, as on the third journey in Asia Minor. Paul's fourth journey, which landed him in the capital of the Roman Empire, would extend the gospel's influence to the entire world.

Later, while in prison again in Rome, Paul looked back on this journey and described it this way in 2 Timothy 4:16:

> At my first defense (before Caesar in Rome on this fourth journey) no one supported me, but all deserted me; may it not be counted against them. But the Lord stood with me and strengthened me, so that through me the proclamation might be fully accomplished, and that all the Gentiles might hear; and I was rescued out of the lion's mouth.[1] (my own comments added in the parentheses)

"All the Gentiles" hearing was quite an amazing feat. The phrase refers to everyone on the planet who was not Jewish. Even if this is a hyperbolic phrase, his fourth journey was certainly profound, with extensive results. How did Paul accomplish so much while being confined to a prison cell, a ship, and an apartment while under house arrest? That is exactly what this chapter will unpack.

Paul's Story: The Fourth Journey

By the end of his third journey, Paul had a depth and variety of experiences few of us can imagine. He had instigated a movement of God that spread rapidly across all of Asia Minor, to the point where every person who lived there heard the message of God. He had fought off wild beasts. He had gone toe-to-toe in spiritual battle with the devil himself. He had preached the gospel in brand new places in Illyricum and had met with many of the churches he had started in previous journeys. He had escaped assassination plots and developed a growing team of Gentile Christian leaders. He had collected a large financial gift to present to the Jerusalem church. All of this was preparation for his greatest missionary journey of all, but one that would have a surprising way of coming to fruition. Luke records this journey in Acts, beginning in chapter 21 and continuing to the end of the book.

Paul's fourth journey began with the return from his third. He shifted from his normal pattern and did not return to Antioch, as he had done with each of the previous journeys. Instead, he went straight to Jerusalem to deliver the relief offering he had collected.

Paul's journeys certainly seem to overlay with Clinton's phases of spiritual maturity nicely (see figure in the Introduction), but that is not to be expected for most people. The stages of our growth in maturity do not always follow the boundaries of well-defined ministry assignments. Job descriptions are not necessarily indicators of our spiritual formation; we may stay in one phase of development while serving in multiple positions and in different settings. Transitioning to another role or location doesn't necessarily mean that we are moving into another stage of ministry maturity. Nevertheless, the characteristics found in each of Paul's journeys are common.

Paul Follows Jesus' Pilgrimage to Jerusalem

Luke uses familiar language to describe Paul's pilgrimage at the beginning of this fourth journey. He says, "Paul purposed in the Spirit to go to Jerusalem" (Acts 19:21). This is very reminiscent of Luke's description of Jesus being "determined to go to Jerusalem" (Luke 9:51). Jerusalem still holds a strong magnetic pull in this world. Jesus and Paul would both ascend to the crescendo of their callings after a determined pilgrimage to the capital of the Promised Land.

The entire time Paul was traveling to Jerusalem, he was given prophetic warnings of what harm would come to him there. Jesus also was aware of the hardships that were awaiting Him at the same destination. With such predictions of suffering, it took purposeful determination to doggedly go there, and that is how Luke describes both of their trips.

Even though it is clear the Holy Spirit was speaking about the bonds and imprisonment that awaited Paul, the message was not necessarily that he should refrain from going. Since Paul already had "purposed in the Spirit" to go, it was simply an opportunity to count the cost of following Christ. He did so emphatically, to the point where he loudly lamented, "What are you doing, weeping and breaking my heart? For I am ready not only to be bound, but even to die at Jerusalem for the name of the Lord Jesus" (Acts 21:13).

Like Jesus, Paul would face his destiny in Jerusalem when the religious Jewish leaders there turned him over to the Gentiles for prosecution. Paul did not know what would happen. Certainly, imprisonment was prophetically foretold, but death was also on the table. What he did know was that Jesus had told him he would speak before kings and rulers (Acts 9:15). This revelation likely gave him a deep confidence in what he was to do, and despite all the prophetic warnings, he pressed on with his band of representatives from the churches of the Gentile world.

Some people think Paul disobeyed the Holy Spirit on this trip, but I think he was simply counting the cost of obedience and rising to the call. The severity of our testing increases with the depth of our maturity (1 Corinthians 10:13). It is doubtful that Paul would have received such a test of his obedience on earlier journeys, but at this point in his life he was equipped to face multiple prophetic warnings from Spirit-filled prophets and still maintain his purpose. It is common to have distractions for our mission arise from the obvious foes of the world, the flesh, and the devil in earlier phases. To face distractions to our mission from Spirit-filled, godly prophets is a much higher test of resolve. The prophets are not to blame—God was speaking to them and using them, just not in the way they suspected at first. This was a test, and Paul passed it. It is what he did once he arrived in Jerusalem that I believe is more questionable.

Paul Enters a Hostile Church Environment

When Paul finally arrived in Jerusalem, he and his companions met with the elders of the Jerusalem church to present the gift they had brought. This mother of all churches had gone through some dramatic changes, however, and most of them were not good.

Earlier in the book of Acts, it had been remarkable that many of the Jewish priests in Jerusalem had become followers of the Way (Acts 6:7). This was good news, of course, but I believe it brought a legalistic bent to the church as well. Although these leaders could agree that Jesus was the promised Messiah, they had no intention of dropping their own Jewish traditions, which unfortunately included belief in a works-based righteousness that focused on temple rituals and circumcision. The church in Jerusalem became a more acceptable thing in the Judaic world. Paul, however, the apostle to the Gentiles, was not acceptable.

Even in the early days of the church's life, there was an undercurrent of religious bigotry in which Jews from Israel held prominence over those who were born outside of Israel (the Hellenistic Jews of Acts 6:1). This prejudice was never addressed but simply accommodated. Rather than blend these two Jewish groups into one, the Jerusalem church created a leadership structure to look after the Hellenists while the twelve apostles and the elders (led by James) cared for the native Jews. To be fair, this bigotry had been inherited and was the product of centuries of cultural persuasion feeding the Jews' feelings of superiority. The influx of priests, highly invested in and committed to the traditional laws, metastasized the spiritual cancer that plagued the Jerusalem church so that animosity toward "others" became normative. In Jerusalem, Hellenistic Jews were second class. Converted Jews and God-fearers (seekers wanting to become Jews) were third class, and all Gentiles were considered wicked and to be hated. The Jerusalem church became in one sense a sect of the Judaism that ruled the city. Paul was not only Hellenistic, but he was the one who spread the good news across the Gentile world without compelling Gentiles to become Jews when they believed. This made him doubly despised and rejected in Jerusalem.

It is far easier, in retrospect, to delineate some of these issues clearly, but at the time there was much confusion. We must remember that little of the New Testament had been written at this point, and it certainly was not put together. The church was just beginning. Suddenly Gentiles were responding to the gospel, and this was often accompanied with obvious signs and wonders. When a Gentile became a Christ-follower, did they also need to become a Jew and obey all the laws of Judaism? To say "no" to such a question was seen as destroying the foundation of all that the Jews believed, and it also seemed to counter the Old Testament commands. So, in their time, it is understandable that these Jewish Christians wanted to hold on to their religion at the expense of people that they already were not fond of.

Here are some questions that may have been burning oxygen in the room:[2]

- Were Gentiles to become Jews and obey all the Torah when they chose to follow the Messiah?
- Were Gentile followers to become part of Israel or not?
- Was circumcision necessary to becoming part of "the faith" (which was Jewish in the eyes of the Jerusalem church)?
- Was the Jesus movement a new faith or simply a sect of Judaism?
- Were Jews to stop living as cultural Jews because of the gospel?
- How much of the Law was a Jew to live by, and how much was no longer relevant because of the Messiah and the salvation He brought?
- How did the Law work to effectively sanctify a believer?
- Which parts of the oral traditions were true, and which, if any, were to be rejected?
- What role did the temple, sacrifices, and rituals play in the life of a follower of Jesus?
- Were there now two ways to be sanctified in Christ—a Jewish way and a Gentile way? Was the church to be divided?
- Were there to be two kinds of Christians with two different paths of spirituality? If so, was Jesus the Savior for both and was the gospel the means of that salvation?

Imagine how hard it would have been to accept Paul's teaching, which was from personal revelation (Galatians 1:11–12), instead of depending on centuries of holy Scripture and the traditions of God's leaders. Paul became a lightning rod in this struggle.

The many Judaic priests who had become part of the Jerusalem church probably felt that they had sure answers for all these questions straight from the Scripture—*and they did*. Even for those who were willing to ignore the Gentile churches, there was no way that God's chosen people were to stop being Jewish or to set aside the Law. The Messiah came to fulfill the Law, not to replace it. Jesus, our Master and model, was Jewish and kept all the Law all the days of His life. The Torah, as the religious Jews understood it, was revelation from God—universal, eternal, and necessary for life and godliness. For many Jews, written law and oral law were hard to separate; Peter himself struggled with this for many years.[3] Some of the hateful views of the Gentiles that were so prevalent in

Judaism seeped into the Jerusalem church and festered there. Paul's work and reputation became an incendiary factor in this situation, and a highly volatile environment was ignited when he arrived.

Paul Bends and Compromises

At this time (around 57 AD), the twelve apostles (the "sent ones") had gone on their various missions, leaving behind the elders of the Jerusalem church, including its leader, James (the Lord's half-brother). James appears to have been balanced in his own views but was fighting an uphill battle trying to keep this church together and healthy. Luke tells us that there were thousands in the Jerusalem church who were said to be "zealous for the law," and who had heard and believed many unkind rumors about Paul. The rumors claimed that Paul was teaching Jews to stop being Jewish and to cease upholding the customs that had been taught to them in Mosaic Law.[4] It is said that a lie will travel halfway around the world before the truth even gets its boots on. People seem wired to believe bad news more easily than good. These were lies being spread about Paul, of course, fabricated by his enemies. Soon Paul became a target of scorn and hatred.

This presented James and the Jerusalem leaders with a quandary. How could they receive a financial gift from someone many of their people considered to be an enemy of God, His Torah, and His chosen people? How could they appease this ugly spirit in a church already compromised in so many ways?

They developed a plan that, I believe, involved some compromise on Paul's part. They asked him to sponsor four Jewish Christians who were trying to complete a Nazirite vow but who, due to some contamination, needed an expensive purification rite in the final seven days of the thirty-day vow.

Sponsoring people to take vows had become a common practice; it was a way for wealthier people to participate in the system of temple devotion (using proxy vow takers) without needing to fulfill the vows themselves. It's unclear why they thought someone could "sacrifice" with other people's money or fulfill a fast with other people's stomachs, but that had become a tradition.

In this case, however, Paul was to not just sponsor these men but also join them in the seven-day cleansing ritual so that afterward the four men could complete the 30-day Nazirite vow they had begun but couldn't afford to finish. The cleansing entailed sacrifices of a lamb, a ram, unleavened bread, cakes of fine flour mixed with oil, and a final offering of meat and drink. During these seven days the men were to live on the temple grounds. This made it prohibitively expensive for the poor Jewish men, and Paul was to step in and cover their costs as well as his own. At the end of the 30-day Nazirite vow, they were to shave their heads and have their hair burned on the altar. The elders' reasoning was that if people saw Paul upholding the Jewish customs, they might realize that the rumors were untrue. In fact, this course of action had the opposite result.

It is easy to miss how significant this decision was for Paul. He must have felt some internal conflict about being asked to compromise on all that he had fought for. Certainly, he saw himself as Jewish, and this custom was part of being Jewish. Paul's conviction was to become under the Law to reach those who were under the Law (1 Corinthians 9:20). There are many commentators who view this as an easy decision that involved no compromise at all. I am not as certain.

This seven-day cleansing ritual would have required Paul to be ceremonially purified from having been in the presence of the "unclean" Gentiles. Given his long years of labor and fellowship with the Gentiles, I imagine this was a very difficult experience. This part of the compromise cost him the most. I believe it would have gone against Paul's heart, the Spirit's leading, and even the truth revealed by God himself. God said concerning the Gentiles, "What I have cleansed, no longer consider unclean" (Acts 10:15). Certainly, Paul could have changed the meaning of the vow in his own head, but the action communicated a message to the rest of the world that was exactly what he had spent his life refuting. We must ask: Is this not a mistake like the one Peter and Barnabas made when they separated themselves from eating with the "unclean" Gentile Christians (Galatians 2:11–14)?

The rest of the Nazirite vow is easily summed up as a symbolic act accompanied by an underlying spiritual devotion. There is nothing about Paul's participation in this that would damage his testimony. Expressing a personal vow in worship and devotion is not bad; Paul had done that himself earlier, without any compromise (Acts 18:18).

From my perspective, this incident may be the low point of Paul's story. It is helpful, however, to realize that even a leader on a fourth journey can make his or her biggest mistake. Let's not assume that just because we are gaining experience and have paid the price to be more mature that we therefore are incapable of making a poor choice in the heat of a precarious moment. It also shows us that there is forgiveness and redemption for mistakes on all the journeys of life. We can finish well even when we make mistakes along the way.

It is important to note that there are a large number of scholars who would disagree with my take on Paul's choice in this situation, and so I want to speak with much caution about it. It is entirely possible that Paul had no hesitation in the act of agreeing to James' plan and saw it simply as personal devotion to God and as a chance to reach out to those "under the Law." He later states to the Sanhedrin in Jerusalem, "I have lived my life with a perfectly good conscience before God up to this day" (Acts 23:1). If you do not agree with my point of view on this, you are in good company, and I am not dogmatically defending my position but merely presenting it as the option that I favor.

Whether or not you believe that Paul acted wrongly, we can agree that his action accomplished next to nothing. It did not further his spiritual sanctification. It did not appease the legalistic Jewish Christians. It did not keep him from being attacked or imprisoned. It was not even this vow that pleased Jesus but rather his uncompromising stance before the Sanhedrin (Acts 23:11). It did, however, give four men a chance to take an expensive vow that they couldn't afford on their own, and so I guess there was some good that came of it.

Near the end of the week, when it seemed that everything might turn out well, pandemonium broke loose. Some Jews from Asia—the place where Paul had experienced his greatest struggle and known his greatest fruitfulness—accused him of defiling the temple. The crowds always seemed to be easily agitated, and soon a violent mob responded to these poisonous lies by seizing and physically assaulting Paul, threatening to kill him. But God had mercy and brought a cohort of Roman soldiers to rescue Paul, sparing his life by preventing his attackers from beating him to death. From this point on in this journey, Paul would be under arrest.

Calm Assurance in Chaotic Direction

The Roman commander who seized Paul had to have him carried away from the vicious mob that was ready to kill him. Ever the opportunist, Paul asked for permission to address the crowd. Luke goes out of his way to show how kind and accommodating the Roman soldiers were to Paul on this journey. At almost every turn, they showed him respect and granted him privileges above and beyond what would have been his due as a prisoner. Therefore, even this strange request of Paul's was granted. In this tense scene, Paul exhibited his artful use of language. He spoke to the Romans in excellent Greek, and he spoke to the Jews in perfect Aramaic. In both cases, his masterful use of the language took his listeners by surprise.

Bloodied and sore from being beaten and now held in bondage, Paul spoke to the crowd from the steps of the Roman barracks, explaining his true heart to the very people who had attempted to tear him to pieces just moments earlier. In love, he announced the good news of Jesus to those who hated him. He started by identifying with his audience in their zeal for the Law. In fact, he told them how he had gone further than they had in his previous pursuit of heretics before Christ interrupted his journey to Damascus nearly thirty years earlier.

Paul spoke about his own true cleansing from sin and his baptism, possibly implying that this religious ritual he had just attempted was useless. Perhaps at this moment he was speaking as much to himself as to the crowd. Emboldened, he went even further and spoke of Jesus' call to him to bring His message to the Gentiles. That was the breaking point. His statement was completely intolerable to the Jewish mob, which began to shout that he was not fit to live. Paul literally turned the other cheek and prayed for those who persecuted him, but he also stood up to their bigotry with great courage. Later, Jesus would tell him that because he had stood so boldly before the Jews, he would be sent to Rome to stand before Caesar himself (Acts 23:11).

There are no journeys we can take where we will not be tested. No matter how mature we become, there is room for growth and tests to show us who we have become.

Once again, like in Philippi, Paul was interrogated by Roman soldiers. But this time Paul was quick to pull out his Roman citizenship credentials before the soldiers could scourge him (Acts 22:25). Then he was brought before the Sanhedrin (the council of Jewish religious leaders composed of the Pharisees and the Sadducees) where he squared off against the high priest. Throughout this proceeding, Paul demonstrated a depth of understanding regarding all the subtleties of what was involved with this group of men, and he used this to his advantage in an impossible situation. Ananias, the high priest, ordered Paul to be struck on the mouth, supposedly for lying. Paul knew this was illegal and responded with authority, calling Ananias a whitewashed wall (of a tomb)! People in the council were shocked, asking, "Do you revile God's high priest?" Paul acknowledged that he should not speak evil of a ruler, and he said he didn't know that Ananias was the high priest. That may have been true, but it may also have been a subtle and sarcastic way of saying, "There is nothing about this man that indicates he is in any way suited to be high priest."

As background, beginning about 170 BC, the Jewish high priests were no longer exclusively drawn from the descendants of Aaron but were appointed by Roman leaders. Ananias, the son of Seth, was appointed high priest by Quirinius, the governor of Syria, in AD 6. He and his family ruled the Sanhedrin for fifty-plus years, with five sons, a son-in-law (Caiaphas), and a grandson all taking turns. That succession included this Ananias, who ordered Paul to be struck (Acts 23:2). Flavius Josephus, in his *Antiquities of the Jews*, says about the family of Ananias: "Now the report goes, that this elder Ananus proved to be a most fortunate man; for he had five sons, who all performed the office of high priest to God, and he had himself enjoyed that dignity a long time formerly, which had never happened to any other of the high priests."[5] It may very well be that Paul was exposing this injustice by saying, "I was not aware, brethren, that he was high priest" (Acts 23:5).

It would normally have been very clear who was the high priest in such a proceeding, and Paul was more than acquainted with the nuances and politics of the Sanhedrin, as well as the family of Ananias. There would have been many signals to indicate which one of the men was in charge. Commentators differ on whether Paul was sincere or sarcastic in this remark; perhaps he was a little of both. Maybe he was assuming that some would think it a sincere comment and not bring any more physical discipline upon him, and at the same time he may have been making a sly comment with his tongue firmly in his cheek. This episode reveals the religious legalism and insider politics that Paul was constantly fighting against. It was not obedience to Mosaic Law that was at issue in this context, for Paul not only quoted the Law but also used it to attack the man who ordered him to be slapped. And then he immediately quoted it again with respect to not speaking evil of one's leaders. It was the oral tradition, which had become law in its application, that had corrupted the leaders and was being used to keep the people oppressed. This dynamic is what Jesus also constantly exposed and countered.

Realizing that no good could come of this meeting, Paul declared himself a Pharisee who was on trial for standing up for the hope of the resurrection of the dead, all of which was true. Since this was a doctrinal difference between the Pharisees and the Sadducees, Paul cleverly got himself out of a precarious place by provoking an argument among his prosecutors, thus revealing just how knowledgeable he was of the Sanhedrin politics. The Roman commander ordered him removed from the bickering group.

On the next night, Jesus appeared beside Paul and said: "Take courage; for as you have solemnly witnessed to My cause at Jerusalem, so you must witness at Rome also" (Acts 23:11). How special this moment must have been to Paul. It was encouragement, enlightenment, empowerment, redemption, and a commissioning from the Lord—all in one simple sentence. Paul was suffering from heinous acts of injustice—lies and fabrications had gotten him arrested without cause. He was being tried on these accusations, yet it was actually Jesus' case, and Paul was merely a witness in the trial. I think sometimes we are a little too full of ourselves at these moments. We feel that it is all about us, we are the victims, and Jesus is just our Comforter. Jesus' words reveal that this is not the way it truly is. Here, Jesus was the one under attack. Let us all remember that it is not our own reputations that are at stake in the missions to which we are called. It is His reputation. The successes and the setbacks are His. It is His rejection, His reception, His redemption—not ours.

These words from Jesus must have taken Paul back thirty years to his vision on the road to Damascus—when he had been the one attacking Jesus. How far he had come. What a difference Jesus had made in his life—and his life was not over. He was to go finally to Rome. He would speak about the risen Lord to kings and rulers. Jesus can say much in just a few words. His Word is powerful on so many levels simultaneously.

No sooner had Jesus spoken these words than Paul's nephew happened to hear of an assassination plot against him. Such plots are not usually broadcast, and so God's hand was certainly evident. Immediately, wheels were set in motion to bring Paul to present the gospel to Caesar, ruler of the mighty Roman Empire, because Jesus had said he would. Jesus' Word is powerful, unbreakable, and fully reliable. In this case, it took immediate effect.

Success Without Trying

Paul was held captive for two years by the Romans in Caesarea, first by Felix (a former slave who had become a Roman ruler), and then by Porcius Festus, who succeeded Felix. The leaders of the Jews in Jerusalem, who were still obsessed with killing Paul, appealed to Festus and requested that Paul be transferred to Jerusalem for trial, planning to ambush him along the way. With that, Paul appealed to be allowed to appear before Caesar, which was his right as a Roman citizen. Festus granted his request. God used the evil intent from murderous assassins to accomplish His stated goal of bringing Paul to Rome where he would present Jesus to Nero himself.

As it turned out, King Agrippa and his wife, Bernice, had come to Caesarea to pay their respects to Festus. When Festus told them about Paul, Agrippa asked to hear from him. Paul boldly declared the gospel to them and was quite persuasive. They could find no reason for Paul to be punished or even imprisoned, but since he had appealed to Caesar, he was sent on his way to Rome.

When Paul set sail for Rome, Luke and Aristarchus (a Macedonian from Thessalonica) were with him. It is possible that they would have had to become slaves of Paul to join him on this voyage. That's one explanation of how Luke was able to be with Paul even in a dungeon when Paul was facing execution (2 Timothy 4:11). Others speculate that Luke was on board as a ship's doctor. Luke doesn't tell us how they were able to accompany Paul; he only informs us that they did.

The first ship they were on left Caesarea and sailed along the coast of Asia and then docked at Myra in current southwest Turkey. Here they changed ships for one bound for Italy. This second ship held 276 people. It was forced by bad weather to stop briefly at Crete.

The harsh winds from the northeast were against them, and despite Paul's warnings, the centurion in charge of the ship insisted that they leave Crete even though winter was approaching. Without sextant or compass, the sailors would have had to rely on the stars for navigation, and so the storm clouds magnified their problems.

The violent winds blew them off course, and the storms prevented the crew from knowing their location. They eventually began to lose hope. They took every measure possible to spare the ship and its passengers, but they were lost at sea and feared being wrecked on the rugged shores of North Africa.

In this scenario, something remarkable happened. Paul, a prisoner, rose to take charge. Aside from the fact that he was a very seasoned traveler who had already been shipwrecked three times, he also had boldness and insight beyond anything the other men had encountered. They not only listened to him but also did all they could to spare the lives of Paul, his companions, and even the rest of the prisoners with them. On the last evening of this ordeal, Paul told them to eat, and he broke bread with them. The language Luke uses to narrate the story is very reminiscent of the language used to describe the Lord's Supper. I believe that Paul took advantage of this moment to present the gospel to these men he had come to know in the midst of great adversity. The next day, the ship ran onto a sandbar off an island, just as the Lord had promised Paul through an angelic messenger. All 276 passengers made it safely to the island of Malta.

Paul, like Jesus, was always a servant and willing to work, and once the soggy crew and passengers were ashore, he began gathering sticks for a fire to warm them up. A disturbed viper, aroused by the fire, emerged from Paul's bundle of wood, struck Paul on the hand, and hung there for all to see. Jesus had told Paul that he would appear before Caesar in Rome. Paul believed what Jesus said, and so, with a flick of the wrist, he disposed of the snake and continued gathering wood. The native people assumed that Paul was evil because he was a prisoner. They thought that this attack was some kind of supernatural punishment for his guilt and that he would die. When there was no sign that the snakebite had hurt Paul, they changed their minds and thought he was a god.

The crew and passengers wintered among the people of Malta, whose leader was Publius. Publius's father was suffering from intense dysentery, and Paul healed him and many others as well. When spring arrived three months later, they resumed their voyage to Rome, amply supplied by the hospitable islanders who were grateful for all Paul had given them.

The rest of the voyage was without incident. Paul was greeted in Rome by a group of Christ-followers who came to honor him. Imagine what the Roman soldiers who had transported this prisoner must have thought of such a greeting. Perhaps by now they had seen enough to know why this man was so loved.

Paul presented the gospel first to the Roman Jews, as was always his pattern. They had not yet heard of him from Jerusalem. After a short time, some were convinced of the truth, but others rejected his message, as had so often been the case.

Paul stayed in Rome for two years, living in rented quarters under house arrest and in the constant presence of a rotation of soldiers who were guarding him. He was given visitation privileges, and people were coming and learning from him all the time. The apartment must have been much more comfortable than a prison cell, but he had to pay the rent, even though he could not leave the apartment to work. Nevertheless, with so many people alongside him, he was not concerned about such things. The Philippian church even sent Epaphroditus with a financial gift to help with his needs (Philippians 4:10–19).

On this fourth journey, Paul unleashed his most powerful gospel work to date, but he couldn't even leave his apartment. Most of us, if we faced the same restraints, would give up on changing the world. We would have every excuse to just pass the time waiting for release. Perhaps some of us with more passionate drive would devote the time to reading or writing, but we would likely lose our motivation and hope of reaching the lost and spreading the gospel movement. Paul did not.

The saying that "all roads lead to Rome" reflects the fact that the Romans established roads, many of them paved, all over the world to connect their vast empire and its trade routes. Thus, in a real sense, Paul was planted in the capital of the world, where paths of influence stretched out in every direction. His apartment became a global headquarters for a Jesus movement that would alter the known world.

Expansion of the Gospel During Paul's Fourth Journey

Today, with computers, the internet, television, and telephones, it is feasible for someone to have an impact on the world and never leave his home, but how did Paul do it back then? Here are seven ways that Paul was able to make such a global impact on his fourth journey:

1. His legal appeal brought his message to key people, such as Felix and his wife, Drusilla; Porcius Festus; King Agrippa and Bernice; and eventually even to Emperor Nero. In fact, it seems as if Paul just kept gaining more and more influence over more and more significant rulers. He went from prefects to regional kings to eventually presenting the gospel to the emperor of the entire Roman Empire.

2. Paul planted the first church of Malta on his way to Rome. He did not even know that such an island existed, and so he hadn't planned on starting a church there. But the Lord of the harvest knew, and it was in His plan. Paul started churches sometimes with only two or three weeks in a place, and so, given his three months on Malta, the gospel might have reached the entire island.

3. Paul's reputation attracted many people to come and hear his message in his rented quarters. He must have had a large apartment, with room for many people. Not only did he have his own team staying with him, but he also entertained many others. (Acts 28:23).

4. Paul's incarceration allowed him to write four epistles that would carry his message throughout the world and across time. While he was in Rome, Paul penned the four letters commonly called

the "prison epistles": Ephesians, Philippians, Colossians, and Philemon. Paul was the apostle to the Gentiles, and in a very real sense he still is. We are still learning from this apostle who changed the world forever by releasing the good news to the Gentile world.

5. Throughout church history, one sure way of spreading the church has been to capture her leaders. Wherever pastors have been killed or locked up, the church has prospered. I'm not sure what that says about church leadership, but this was true even in Paul's time. His detention and restriction provoked others to take up his mission because it was assumed that he no longer could do it (Philippians 1:14–18).

6. During his stay in Rome, Paul had access to lost people that the church could probably not have reached otherwise. That sounds strange. What people would he have had access to if he couldn't leave his own apartment? Well, you might say he had a captive audience. All day, every day, there was a Roman soldier no more than a couple of steps from him (Acts 28:16). The Romans were outstanding military strategists. They knew that to keep a soldier alert on his watches, it was necessary to rotate assignments to keep his attention sharp and avoid complacency. One day a guard would be beside Paul, receiving teaching on the life of Jesus, and the next day he might be protecting the emperor's daughter. While Paul was under house arrest, he wrote to the Philippians that all who were in Christ in Rome sent their greetings, especially those of Caesar's own household (Philemon 4:22). The gospel had spread virally and even infiltrated the palace into Nero's own *oikos*. Legend has it that some of Nero's own family members were executed for following Christ. The soldiers who guarded Paul took the message of Jesus to other places as well—all over the Roman Empire. They were missionaries sent by and paid by Rome.

I like to think that Paul took advantage of his writing a letter to the Ephesians to open a conversation about the gospel when a new soldier came on guard duty. I imagine Paul busily writing a letter, then stopping, looking to his side. He would scan up and down the soldier, then write some more: *Belt of truth*. Then he would look back at the soldier again and go immediately back to writing: *Helmet of salvation.* He would continue, giving the soldier another look, and then write more. Eventually the soldier would ask him what he was writing. I envision Paul saying, "I am describing the most powerful soldier in the world today." The soldier was probably flattered and stood more upright with a look of pride. Paul would shake his head, and say, "Oh, it's not you. I'm just using you as a model. The soldier I'm writing about can fight off evil spirits of all kinds and not lose ground." I imagine that Paul's guard was so intrigued that he eventually enlisted in the kind of army Paul was describing.

7. Paul was always mentoring new leaders and sending them out to reproduce his ministry and multiply his influence around the world. Both Acts and the prison epistles mention many people who were with Paul during his imprisonment, including Epaphroditus, Timothy, Luke, Mark, Demas, Aristarchus, Jesus (called Justus), Epaphras, Tychicus, and Onesimus. We can assume that there were even more who were not mentioned, including the soldiers. These disciples of Jesus, empowered and mentored by Paul, would strike out across the world on the roads radiating from Rome to do works like those that Paul had done on his earlier journeys.

   Paul multiplied Christ-followers. Where once there was only one team, made up of Barnabas and Saul, now there were multiple teams being sent off all over the world. This is how Paul could say, "…that through me the proclamation might be fully accomplished, and that all the Gentiles might hear" (2 Timothy 4:17).

   Luke's narrative ends with Paul's imprisonment in Rome. This was the end of the book of Acts, but not the end of Paul's journeys.

Your Story: Lessons of the Fourth Journey

In Clinton's phases of maturity toward finishing well that we have consistently referenced, this fourth journey would best be described as *afterglow.* The few who get to this stage in any generation have unusual spiritual authority that is apparent to everyone and that tends to reach far and wide in their world. Ministry comes to them, and they don't have to go looking for it. They plan less and simply step into what God has for them. If *convergence* is where all their experience, gifts, and lessons come together for a productive season (Paul's third journey), *afterglow* is where it shines globally for all to see. I refer to the rare individual who reaches this phase of growth as a fourth-journey person.

Most Christians will never get to the fourth journey. This is not a tragedy, just an obvious truth. The many who don't make it this far are not necessarily incomplete or failures. The fourth journey is a rare gift for only a few in each generation.

The Secret of Contentment

The fourth-journey person cares less about daily provisions than he or she used to. Fourth-journey people no longer write support letters or wonder about how they will pay the rent. Paul wrote from his rented quarters to the Philippians that he had learned the secret of contentedness in any circumstance (Philippians 4:10-14). He thanked them for their financial gift but also told them he didn't need it. He was more excited about the blessing that giving had brought to them than about what it had brought to him. He knew God had called him to Rome, and so it was up to God to get him there and provide while he was there. And God did.

Paul also said in that passage of the Philippian letter that he was just as satisfied in poverty as he was in prosperity. In any and all circumstances he had learned the secret to contentment. Oh, how things would change if that attitude were more common among followers of Jesus. When insecurity and striving after things are removed, fourth-journey people stand as almost invincible against the enemy. You cannot buy these people; you cannot even punish them. As we see with Paul, imprisonment only fuels their mission.

This contentedness is a powerful and attractive quality. It makes fourth-journey people not just at peace and full of joy but also without insecurity. In that sense, they are undefeatable. Enemies will find that the usual ploys of temptation, deception, slander, and threats carry little weight against someone who has reached the afterglow of the fourth journey.

Paul had nothing to lose because he already gained all he ever needed or wanted in Jesus. Compared with Christ, nothing lured or enticed him.

People in the afterglow stage don't sweat the small stuff, and everything is small compared with the overwhelming sufficiency of Jesus.

Sought Out by the World's Influencers

The fourth-journey person's reputation can increase even in the eyes of the world's leaders. Because Paul faithfully pursued Christ though every trial, eventually he had audiences with governors, kings, and emperors. Paul's spiritual authority was so great that a Roman soldier took the advice of this fourth-journey *prisoner* when facing a life-or-death crisis on an ill-fated voyage. The soldier listened to Paul rather than the counsel of his fellow soldiers or even professional sailors. A fourth-journey person's authority is evident for all to see.

While few in any generation reach this phase, there are many examples over the course of history of people who found themselves in the fourth journey. When the patriarch Abraham was in afterglow and found that God provided for his needs, he stopped seeking after possessions. Joseph found that his own difficult trials produced in him spiritual authority that Pharoah would seek out; and he fulfilled his destiny that had been revealed at a younger age. Daniel found that world rulers sought his wisdom and direction, and he stopped caring about provisions, positions, or rewards. Patrick of Ireland eventually found that his ministry spread farther than he could imagine, and his apprentices took his work far beyond where he ever traveled. George Whitefield found a groove where tens of thousands came to hear his message, including some of the greatest leaders of US history, such as Benjamin Franklin. John Wesley is famous for his hard work and many long journeys on horseback, but more churches were started after his death than while he was alive. Perhaps the closest comparison to Paul's fourth journey would be how Watchman Nee saw his work flourish the most after he was imprisoned by the Chinese communists.

Many of God's people live lives in humble obscurity. I am convinced that the bones of some of the greatest heroes of God's Kingdom are now buried under unmarked and unremarkable graves. They are unknown here and now and may not ever have been famous—but they will be greatly honored in the next life.

Do not think that you must become a celebrity to reach a fourth journey. And certainly don't think that real success is to become famous. Real success is to find out what God wants of you and to do it with faith beyond any realistic expectation—to your last breath. But those few who grow into a fourth journey typically are recognized and even sought out by contemporaries for the wisdom they have gained over all their life journeys. The difference between those who are in an earlier journey and those in the fourth is this: the fourth-journey person isn't impressed by worldly powerbrokers who seek their insight, and they don't take themselves too seriously either. The trap and seduction of fame is less a concern to those on their fourth journey. They are so enamored with Jesus that *everyone* else is just a person who needs Jesus—nothing more and nothing less. The fourth-journey person is as interested in a runaway slave like Onesimus as they are in Nero, the emperor of the world.

No Worries about Circumstances

The fourth journey brings expansive influence beyond what expectations or circumstances would predict. On his third journey, Paul took three years to reach a single region of Asia Minor, and he was free not only to teach in the school of Tyrannus but also to move about from house to house and work with his hands in the marketplace. On this, his last but most effective journey, he was confined to his apartment for only two years, and yet he was able to reach the Gentile world because others took his message for him (2 Timothy 4:16-17). By doing "less," he did more.

Paul had been imprisoned before this. People on earlier journeys can sometimes find themselves in a type of prison or limitation, but they usually look to have influence only in the immediate surrounding. They are unable to envision that their confinement is an evidence of God's sovereign plan to advance His Kingdom globally. It takes the experience of seeing God work over many years to be at a place to find such an oppressive confinement to be an opportunity.

Paul, in spite of many prophetic words about his arrest and imprisonment, did not seek in any way to take an easier path. He was following Christ, believing in Christ, and going wherever His Master said to go. If that meant being bound in chains, then chains were somehow going to bring the gospel to the nations.

Fourth-journey Christ-followers no longer get stressed over their work. By this time, these people have become comfortable in their own skin, and they allow the work to flow naturally from their character and intimacy with Christ (Galatians 2:20). They find success without really trying. Success comes to them, not the other way around. They have confidence that God will do the work that He always intended to accomplish, and they do not feel compelled to try to force it to happen.

The Greater the Maturity, the Greater the Temptations

The fourth-journey person still faces life tests and continues to experience character growth. The battles we face against the world, the flesh, and the devil will last throughout our lifetimes. Those who make it to the fourth journey are not immune to the challenges to their character. In fact, often the temptations of a fourth-journey disciple may be subtle but much more intense. As we become stronger in Christ, the temptations also increase in strength and trickery, such that fourth-journey Christ-followers may face their greatest challenges at a stage where they may be inclined to let down their defenses. A young Jesus faced the devil three times after spending forty days fasting in the desert, but I believe His single night in Gethsemane was a far more challenging test. Just because we are more mature and less easily deceived doesn't mean the tests get easier. No, it means that the tests are at an even higher level of pressure.

On his fourth journey Paul was attacked by a mob, falsely accused, threatened with death, had assassins plot to kill him, was shipwrecked, bitten by a viper, and incarcerated—and handled all these circumstances with grace. His response was not at all thrown off by a concern for himself. But on this journey Paul might have committed his greatest mistake when he gave in to the pressure of taking a public vow. The temptation he faced was not to save himself, it was to take a questionable action to make sure the financial gift he was bringing from all his spiritual children would be received for its intended purpose. He risked his personal convictions to make certain the blessing that came from the sacrifice of the children he loved so much would not be in vain. He chose to cleanse himself publicly for having been among the unclean because of his great love for his children in the faith—the very people thought to be unclean by the Jews. That's a much higher level of pressure.

It is wonderful news that redemption is as readily available to fourth-journey people as to any others. It is tempting for naïve believers to think that the more mature they become, the less sin is a problem. A fourth-journey person would laugh at this idea. The temptations of sin do not evaporate for mature Christ-followers. Because the mature saint has built up more resistance to normal patterns of temptation, the enemy must up his game and use all his cunning to attack.

My ministry partner Dezi Baker often chides people by asking why they do not face greater temptations in their lives. His answer? "Because most sell out for chump change." God will not allow us to face temptations that we lack the ability to resist (1 Corinthians 10:13). A lack of engagement with our enemy may indicate a lack of robustness in our ability to resist. Fourth-journey people are on guard against the devil's blatant and subtle attacks. They are acutely aware that they need the gospel as much near the end of their lives as they ever did at the beginning, and they will be the first to tell you so.

Writing Books that are Read by Generations to Come

The fourth journey is when leaders often expand their written influence so that countless people benefit from their experience and wisdom. Some leaders get absorbed with writing too soon, and their learning dwindles as they become "experts." The great writers continue growing and learning. Fourth-journeyers write books that are read for generations, not simply for a season. The authority behind their words comes from the hard-won lessons of enduring all the previous journeys.

A glance at any bestseller list may discover some good reads. But a look over the classics shelf will reveal a wholly different kind of book. These are the books that are read decades, lifetimes, even centuries removed from when they were written. Their writers have thoughts and words that carry universal meaning not bound by culture or fad.

Paul wrote thirteen New Testament epistles that remain in our Bibles. Of all that he wrote, I believe there are only two that seem to not be written to address a particular problem in a specific church—Ephesians and Colossians, which are broader in their intent. During Paul's fourth journey, his writing took on a far more universal direction. I'm not suggesting that his other letters were not applicable to all; he wrote to Timothy that "All scripture is inspired by God and profitable…" (2 Timothy 3:16). But it was during Paul's fourth journey that he felt an authority to write literally for the entire world and all the ages to come.

Onesimus, Lasting Fruit of the Fourth Journey

To demonstrate Paul's fourth-journey impact, I would like to take a closer look at Onesimus, one of the men mentioned as being with the apostle in his Roman imprisonment. I believe his story best illustrates what was going on in Paul's apartment in Rome and how that influenced so many places in the world. Much of what I am about to write is my speculation based on the facts we know from the New Testament accounts, but it does illustrate what I believe was happening while Paul was on this journey.

Onesimus had been born into slavery in Asia Minor. He wanted freedom more than anything else, even family, and so one day he stole some items from his master and ran away. A runaway slave had no rights, and if caught he would have received a severe punishment, not only to teach him a lesson but also to set an example for all other slaves. The Roman Empire was built on slavery, and runaways could not be tolerated.

Wanting to start a new life, Onesimus decided that the best place to not be noticed was in a big city. In a small town, he couldn't blend in and remain anonymous. Perhaps in Rome he could. Once he was in Rome, he found that he was not free at all. He could never trust anyone enough to reveal who he really was. He was afraid of being caught, and he was lonely because any close relationship was built on lies. Finding decent work was difficult without references. Every time he saw a Roman soldier, his heart would beat faster and adrenalin would course through his body. No, he was less free than when he served as a slave under his master.

Somehow, Onesimus heard that the apostle Paul was in town and welcoming visitors. He remembered the difference that Paul's message had made to his old master, Philemon, and was intrigued by the thought of meeting the apostle. One day Onesimus awoke in desperation, still longing for that illusive freedom. He decided that this day he would finally be free—or he would be dead. I speculate that he made this decision because he chose to walk into the presence of a Roman guard and spill his guts to Paul. You can't imagine how dangerous this was. This could have resulted in immediate seizure and punishment, perhaps even public execution. Nevertheless, he went. He was that desperate.

Fortunately, the soldier guarding Paul that day had become a follower of Christ and looked the other way. Onesimus chose to follow Jesus and for the first time in his life found true freedom. He was immediately discipled by Paul, who put him to work right away. With his new freedom, Onesimus found that he had a reason to live and serve, and so he became very useful to Paul. I imagine being his authentic self around others added to his enthusiasm.

After some time of training, Paul realized that Onesimus would have to reconcile his past with his master, Philemon, before he could develop further. Therefore, Paul wrote two letters, one to Philemon and one to the church that met in Colossae in Philemon's home. He may have also included the Laodicean letter (Colossians 4:16) at this time as well, since Laodicea was a neighboring town (Colossians 2:1; 4:13-16). With the epistles packed in his bag, Onesimus embraced Paul and his companions and went on his own first journey as a disciple. When he came into familiar country near Colossae, he awoke one morning and decided again that on this day he would be either free or dead—a decision that we all must learn to make daily. He was about to enter the home of his former master and turn himself in.

I picture that at the moment when the two came face to face, Onesimus quickly handed the letters to his master and bowed very low to the ground. I see Philemon reading the letters and granting Onesimus his freedom. We can read about that in the second chapter of Philemon. Well, actually, there is no second chapter of the letter to Philemon. But the letter itself, by its very existence, does tell us a story. If Philemon had chosen to not liberate Onesimus, we can be confident that he would not have circulated the letter that today is included in the canon of the New Testament. It is safe to assume Onesimus was set free by Philemon.

There is nothing more said about either Philemon or Onesimus in the Bible, but there is a historical document that mentions Onesimus. In a letter written by Ignatius of Antioch roughly thirty years after John wrote the book of Revelation to the Ephesian church and her sister churches of Asia Minor, Onesimus is mentioned.

This letter is illuminating for us on two levels. First, it answers a question for us about what became of Onesimus; secondly, it also answers a question about what became of the Ephesian church.

The New Testament does not close with a good word about this highly influential church. In Revelation, Jesus dictates a letter to John for the church and described it as sound in its doctrine and intolerant of false apostles but said she had lost something of utmost importance—her first love. Jesus told the church to repent or be removed from His presence (Revelation 2:1-7). With that, the Bible ends its discussion of the Ephesian church. That is not a happily-ever-after kind of ending.

But here are the words of Ignatius to the Ephesians:

> I gave a godly welcome to your church which has so endeared itself to us by reason of your upright nature, marked as it is by faith in Jesus Christ, our Savior, and by the love of Him. You are imitators of God; and it was God's blood that stirred you up once more to do the sort of thing you do naturally and have now done to perfection. …In God's name, therefore, I received your large congregation in the person of Onesimus, your bishop in this world, a man whose love is beyond words. My prayer is that you should love him in the Spirit of Jesus Christ and all be like him. Blessed is He who let you have such a bishop. You deserved it![6]

Judging from Ignatius' letter, the Ephesian church was stirred up again and returned to her first love, and a new age of fruitfulness was born. Jesus once said that the one who is forgiven much, loves much (Luke 7:47). It took the influence of a man like Onesimus, who knew firsthand what forgiveness was all about, to stir this church up once more to the love of Christ. The runaway slave not only found the freedom he so desperately wanted but also started on his own journeys that ended with his taking a leadership role in one of the most influential churches of the first century. The fruit of Paul's fourth journey endured in the lives of the people he mentored.

Fourth-Journey Reflections

It will be rare indeed for someone reading this book to be in his or her fourth journey, but if that is a possibility, here are some reflection questions to ask yourself:

- Are the temptations you face becoming much more challenging because your level of resistance is also increasing? Is Satan having to up his game in the conflict between you two? In what ways?
- Are you less concerned about where your finances come from than you were previously?
- Do people who are not even in our faith recognize spiritual power in you and come to you for advice?
- Is the audience for your writing or speaking increasing, even extending internationally? Do your trained apprentices take your work to the ends of the earth? Do circumstances seem to be insurmountable, and yet the greatest progress of your mission occurs from that situation? Do you find that whatever you do, your mission advances without you even trying?

There was one more journey left for Paul, and it would become the capstone of his life. This is a journey that we all must make, but we do not all make it as well as Paul. Let's rededicate ourselves to finishing well with passion and perseverance.

CHAPTER 7

THE FINAL JOURNEY

Choose Now How You Would Finish

If Christianity is anything at all, it is an exercise in willingness.
—Dezi Baker

*The time of my departure has come. I have fought the good fight,
I have finished the course, I have kept the faith.*
—Paul at the end of his life (2 Timothy 4:7)

My brother and I were born less than a year apart. When we were in middle school, we went with our mother on an adventure most young boys only dream about—a safari to East Africa. Anything but tame, the trip featured close encounters with wild animals of all sorts.

Our journey took us first to Treetops, a hotel on stilts that overlooked a water hole. Wild animals would come from miles around to drink as we tourists observed them from above. Of course, we were not the first ones to have had this view—the monkeys and baboons had been living in the treetops long before any reservations were made at that hotel. When we checked in, we were warned to keep our windows closed so that these curious forest dwellers didn't steal our possessions while we were asleep. The primates were so at home at Treetops that they would mingle with the guests, sometimes reaching right into their bags to take shiny objects such as cameras or glasses. I learned, however, not to assume that these animals were tame simply because they were comfortable near people.

The morning after we arrived, I was on the top platform and saw a gray baboon reach into a woman's purse to steal her camera. He was close enough for me to touch him, and I was foolish enough to do so. I grabbed his tail, just for an instant, and in a flash the animal spun around screaming, mouth wide open. I saw teeth that seemed to grow longer and sharper as his mouth opened wider. I quickly let go of the baboon's tail and froze with fear. The baboon took the camera and left. I'm surprised he didn't take a picture of the dumb look on my face to give the rest of his troop a good laugh.

From Treetops we traveled to the Maasai Amboseli Game Reserve. Our tour guide, hearing about my previous encounter, decided to play a joke on me. He told me that the rhesus monkeys at our next stop were friendly toward tourists. When I tried to approach a monkey beside a tree, it shrieked at me. I stepped back, and, seeing my timidity, the monkey courageously filled the gap I left. Before I knew it, monkeys were dropping out of the tree above to surround me, all of them screaming, and I took off running, chased by a gang of simian hoodlums.

That evening I was not very hungry and stayed in our bungalow while my mother and brother went up to the lodge for dinner. About dessert time, I had a remarkable recovery and decided to walk up to the lodge just after dark. There were usually zebras or impalas grazing on the lawn in the evening, but that night there were none to be found. This seemed unusual, but since everything I was seeing was unusual, I didn't think much of it.

The lights inside the dining area were glowing, and I could see all the people inside, but none were at their tables. They were all pressed up against the windows—looking at me! They were also waving at me. Some seemed to be urging me to return to my bungalow, and others appeared to want me to hurry up and get inside. I had no clue as to why they were gesturing, but I quickened my pace. Once inside, I was told that a leopard was out in the grass, stalking me. Fortunately, the sharpshooters had their rifles trained on her in case she wanted a little dessert herself. I remember wondering how many kids at my school could boast that a leopard had stalked them during summer vacation.

Within a couple of weeks, I had seen cheetahs, lions, giraffes, elephants, and hordes of wildebeest. I had tried to catch foot-long lizards and had been bitten by more flies than Steven King could use in a horror movie.

At our last stop, I watched my brother feed a tall, multicolored crested crane, which looked as if it had a punk rock haircut made of feathers. It lived in the hotel lobby where tourists could buy seeds for a few coins and feed it. I figured I could handle this, but by now my reputation had spread throughout the animal kingdom. As I approached, that bird squawked menacingly at me and advanced with its long neck and sharp beak. Startled, I stepped back, and it came after me. My mother watched the long-legged crane chase me through the lobby, leaving my brother in peace.

I tell you this story of my childhood journey in Africa because it has a lesson about life. My brother and I were about the same age and had the same upbringing. But whereas I came home from that trip lucky to have all my fingers but also with lots of stories to tell, my brother had spent most of the trip reading a novel about adventures in Africa.

There are people in the world who live the adventure, and there are those who merely read about others' adventures. I determined a long time ago that I wasn't going to be someone who only read about the adventures of others. I would live the kind of life people would want to read about. And I want a life full of gusto, with a go-for-it faith that risks everything on the belief that God is indeed real and will carry me through to the end. As I grow older, I do not want to stagnate but instead to see my life get even more meaningful. I want my last lap to be my best lap in this life-long race.

The apostle Paul lived the kind of life that others would write about. By studying the journeys of Paul, we have learned much about the elements that go into the spiritual formation of someone who makes a lasting difference. Let's now look at how he finished.

Paul's Story: The Final Journey

We have no scriptural account and very little dependable evidence about what happened after Paul's first Roman imprisonment that is recorded at the end of Acts. Nevertheless, we can piece some information together from the pastoral epistles (written after his fourth journey) and a few other historical documents.

After his release from Rome, Paul may have gone to Spain, as he had indicated he intended to do (Romans 15:23–29). The first-century Christian leader Clement seems to indicate (1 Clement 5:6–7) that Paul preached as far as the limits of the West, which was likely Spain.[1]

Paul's time in the West could not have been long, since during this brief time of freedom he was also in Crete, initiating new works and leaving Titus there to oversee them (Titus 1:5). From Crete, Paul and Timothy may have started traveling toward Macedonia, but Timothy stayed in Ephesus to address some problems in the church (1 Timothy 1:3). This was prior to the letter Jesus authored to that church (Revelation 2:1-7), so perhaps Paul and Timothy could envision the growing problems that needed correction.

Paul went on to Macedonia and while there wrote 1 Timothy and Titus. Paul spent a winter in Nicopolis (Titus 3:12), and it's likely that he was headed back to Ephesus when he was arrested in Troas (2 Timothy 4:13–15), perhaps betrayed by a man named Alexander.

A short time after he wrote to Titus, Paul was deserted by Demas, who "loved this present world" (2 Timothy 4:10). On his way to Rome after his arrest in Troas, Paul must have stopped in Miletus and Corinth (2 Timothy 4:20) where some of his associates remained, for reasons far more favorable than those given for his separation from Demas.

Paul's arrest eventually landed him in a dungeon in Rome, where he wrote his last letter, which we call 2 Timothy. This imprisonment was to be his last. In AD 66, Paul was beheaded.

After traveling 15,000 miles (8,700 by land), enduring four shipwrecks, starting churches in seven or eight people groups, writing fifteen letters that we know of (thirteen of which are in the New Testament), and enduring multiple imprisonments and uncounted beatings, Paul ended his life almost alone.[2]

According to 2 Timothy, he spent his last days short on time (4:9), cold (4:13), lonely (4:11), rejected by his own spiritual children (1:15), abandoned by his son in the faith (4:10), and betrayed (4:14). Nevertheless, even though few stood with him in the end, he was a success (4:6–8). My friend and mentor Bob Logan defines success as finding out what God wants you to do and doing it. If indeed that is success, then Paul finished very well. But Paul's fruitfulness did not end when his physical life did. Not at all. His ministry continues to this day, to this very chapter you are reading at this moment.

As Paul's days came to a close, he was most concerned that his spiritual children would carry on the work. In his letter to his spiritual son Timothy he wrote, "You therefore, my son, be strong in the grace that is in Christ Jesus. The things which you have heard from me in the presence of many witnesses, entrust these to faithful men who will be able to teach others also" (2 Timothy 2:1-2). Paul's influence continues to multiply for generations.

Those Paul mentored—Timothy, Luke, Titus, Mark, Aristarchus, Epaphras, Onesimus, Epaphroditus, and many more—continued the work he began. In fact, the work multiplied faster and further after he died than during his life. That is finishing well.

Your Story: Preparing for Your Final Journey

On a drive in Los Angeles one day, I heard a radio ad for a mortuary. It asked, "If you should ever die, will your family be prepared?" There is no "if" in this equation but only "when," and for most of us, the "when" is not known in advance. George Bernard Shaw once quipped, "One out of one people die. That's a startling statistic!" The question is not whether you will die, but whether you will live well.

Unlike Paul, we will not all be blessed to experience a third or fourth journey—some will fall away, some will plateau, and some will die while on earlier journeys. There are no guarantees of these breakthrough seasons of a life lived well. But there is a guarantee that every one of us will experience this final journey. The question isn't whether it will happen but how you will be prepared when it does.

The Corruption of Christian Leadership: From a Prison to a Palace

I visited Rome a few years ago with my daughter Heather, and we went to the Mamertine Prison, which is also called Paul's Prison. This is where, at the end of his life, Paul is believed to have written 2 Timothy. We descended into the prison which had stone walls, floor, and ceiling with no windows. The space was so claustrophobic my head grazed the ceiling when I stood upright. Heather and I looked at each other in the prison's dim light, with the smell of mildew in our nostrils, and I realized that this was probably the very place where God had inspired Paul to compose that letter to Timothy, which is one of my favorite books of the Bible. In this tiny space, Paul had agonized over his few remaining days and the lasting impact of his life. He had been here just hours before he was walked to the place of his execution, when his vibrant soul was transferred into the light of God's eternal presence.

What a contrast with the Vatican, which we visited later the same day. Great historical riches adorn the Papal Palace and the rest of this religious city. The ceiling of the Sistine Chapel is too high to touch, but we would never have been permitted to do that—the chapel's ceiling is the famous masterpiece by Michelangelo. In the passage of history, it is not that long of a time between Paul living out his last moments in prison to when Christian leaders were honored by men and lived like kings in the pope's palace. The deterioration of Christendom's leaders' fortitude and character is quite evident between these two places. Though their reputation and socioeconomic class improved greatly, an obvious decay is on display when you consider the heart of the leaders.

Paul was surrounded by unforgiving stone, while most popes are surrounded by wealth, power, and prestige. But how many popes' names do you remember? Paul and his legacy are better remembered—and always will be.

Both sites—the Vatican and the Mamertine Prison—impressed me deeply. Books of the Bible have been written in places like the Vatican but also in dungeons, or by authors who were on the run in the wilderness with pursuers breathing down their necks.[3] Daniel and Joseph were God's servants who took their final journey from a soft bed in a spectacular palace, proving it possible, though rare.

My art background had drawn me to the Vatican, but my heart never left the cave of Paul's prison. Standing there trying to imagine Paul in that place at the end of such an amazing life gave me insights that impact me to this day.

I couldn't help asking myself in which of these two places I would prefer to end my days. Most of us would choose the elegance and power of the palace over the isolation of a death row prison cell. In one place people would admire and revere us, and in the other we would be forgotten and assumed to be a criminal.

Western culture exalts people who are rich, beautiful, and skilled—whether performers, influencers, politicians, or athletes—regardless of their character. Nevertheless, the people with the greatest spiritual significance do not usually come from places of comfort and privilege but from situations of hardship and great challenge. Those who finish strong have the toughness of Christ-like character forged under the pressure of great adversity. While the pope rules a global religious empire from the Vatican and Paul was alone but for Luke, if I had to choose, it would be to finish well in the dungeon.

Finishing well in obedience to God is better than finishing comfortable. Greater comfort than we could ever imagine is just a blink away from our final breath (Romans 8:18). We would do well to focus our eyes there.

Succession is the Greatest Success

A prime characteristic of the ministry of those who faithfully exercise the spiritual gift of apostleship is succession. Because apostles empower those around them, they can start a work and move on in God's appropriate timing. When they do leave, the work left behind excels.

Paul wrote about this to the Philippians: "…just as you have always obeyed, not as in my presence only, but now *much more* in my absence…" (Philippians 2:12, emphasis added). And Jesus, the archetypal apostle, said to His disciples: "It is to your advantage that I go away, for the Father will send the Holy Spirit…and greater works will you do than I do" (my paraphrase). This strategy of raising up competent successors has been lacking in organized religion for the past few centuries. It is because we have minimized and marginalized the apostolic gift that succession is so rarely done well. This is something every leader should be concerned with.

The late leadership guru Peter Drucker once remarked, "There is no success without a successor." Since the building of the Vatican, succession has often become associated with filling job titles rather than reproducing

Christ in others. We simply must bring back the true expression of the apostolic gifting. Any leader can and should be intentional about finding a successor. Unfortunately, most do not even consider that responsibility until it is too late. You don't have to be an apostle to pass the baton well, but it becomes much easier and more normative when the apostolic foundation of church is well established.

While Paul lay in a dungeon awaiting his execution, he still finished well. What happened after his death is perhaps more remarkable than all he did alive. As I remarked above, Paul said, "The things you heard from me…entrust to faithful men who will be able to teach others also" (2 Timothy 2:2). There are four generations of workers in this simple admonition: Paul to Timothy, Timothy to faithful men, and faithful men to others also. Ultimately you and I are the "others also." The life of Jesus has come down through the centuries to us. We must not drop the baton but pass it on well to the next generation. Paul accomplished this. Will we?

Finish Well or Die Trying

J. Robert Clinton, one of the scholars on whose shoulders I stand as I write this book, and whom I cite in almost every chapter, states that only one in three leaders in the Bible finished well. That, in and of itself, is sobering, but his next words are even more shocking. After studying the lives of thousands of leaders, he goes on to say that one in three is too generous an estimate for the number of leaders who finish well today.[4]

We can conclude that finishing well is not easy, not common, and not celebrated enough. It must be a choice that we make, perhaps even a vow we declare before God. It should be so important to us that it takes precedence over other factors that most people become content with. Popularity, material success, goals achieved, comfortable retirement, travel, selling a business, having family that love you—these are all good things, but they are not what finishing well is ultimately about. In the end, and it is only discovered there, finishing well is between you and God. It is about continuing to learn and grow and never stopping your curiosity and love of Jesus and His world. Finishing well is about your love of God being the most important core of your being and never letting it be tampered with or forgotten. When the time comes and the curtain falls, you will be alone before God, and that is when you discover if you did indeed fight the good fight, keep the faith, and finish the race.

In high school, I had the privilege of being a member of a very competitive swim team. We were good enough to win, and everyone in Los Angeles expected that we would. We had just one rival in our league that had a shot at defeating us—the Westchester High team. Before the city finals took place, we faced these opponents at the earlier league finals. Our team was waiting to peak at the city championships, and so we had not prepared as well as we could have—and Westchester knew it. They had worked hard to be at their very best at the league finals, hoping to beat us there before our peak. Our rivals swam better than anyone expected them to, and they went head-to-head with us through all the events. The league championship finally came down to the last race—an all-out sprint by our four fastest swimmers in the 200-yard freestyle relay.

Our team had a secret weapon; his name was Zach. He was the fastest sprinter in the league. Unfortunately, he had injured his shoulder earlier in the year, and though he had worked hard to get back in shape and make up for lost time, he had missed many meets. All the training he had been able to do since his injury was for this one moment.

Zach rose to the challenge. He dove in after the third leg of the relay and swam with no hesitation, no reservations, no thought at all except to touch the wall before his opponent. He gave it everything he had and moved clearly into first place. In the last few strokes, his shoulder popped out of its socket, but Zach swam through the pain and touched the wall first. Everyone in the stands was cheering, and the noise in the natatorium was so loud that my skin was vibrating!

We won! We won the relay, the meet, and the league championship. The year was ours! All the sacrifice and early-morning workouts had paid off. In one glorious moment of struggle and endurance, our team had pulled together and tasted victory.

In the thrill of the moment and without thinking, one of my teammates jumped into the water to embrace Zach and help lift him out of the pool. But one of the other teams had not yet finished the race, and so our team was automatically disqualified because of this spontaneous act, even though it was done with the best intentions. I will never forget the sinking feeling that came over all of us as we realized what had happened. It spread across the spectators like a cold wave.

We lost! We lost the relay, the meet, and the league championship. Through one moment of thoughtless emotional reaction, our team tasted the bitterness of defeat and disgrace. All the sacrifice, all the hard work, and all the year's effort came down to a crashing defeat.

The return trip from the meet was the quietest bus ride I had ever been on. The air seemed to have been sucked out of our lungs. We could barely breathe, let alone speak. We had nothing to say anyway.

The analogy is obvious. What could be more disastrous than working hard all our life to win only to be disqualified at the very end? The apostle Paul was not disqualified. Alone and about to die, he finished a success in every sense that mattered. He determined early in his life that he would finish well.

At the end, Paul was likely more infamous than famous and known more for his jail time than his journeys. That would change in all the succeeding generations, but in his own time, he likely felt forgotten by all but a few people. Nevertheless, he knew he fought the good fight, he finished the course, and he kept his faith. There was a crown awaiting that would fit his head, and his alone.

Finding the Faith to Win in the End

Eugene Peterson, who gave us *The Message*, has a book that takes its title, curiously, from a passage in *Beyond Good and Evil* by Friedrich Nietzsche—the famous atheist who declared that God is dead. The title of Peterson's book is *A Long Obedience in the Same Direction*, and here are Nietzsche's words: "The essential thing 'in heaven and earth' is . . . that there should be a long obedience in the same direction; there thereby results, and has always resulted in the long run, something which has made life worth living."

Paul viewed his life as a great race, and he exemplified a long obedience in a single direction. He wrote to the Corinthians:

Do you not know that those who run in a race all run, but only one receives the prize? Run in such a way that you may win.

Everyone who competes in the games exercises self-control in all things. They then do it to receive a perishable wreath, but we an imperishable. Therefore I run in such a way, as not without aim; I box in such a way, as not beating the air; but I buffet my body and make it my slave, so that, after I have preached to others, I myself will not be disqualified. (1 Corinthians 9:24–27)

At the beginning of any race, everyone stands and applauds as the gun fires and the runners dash forward. Everyone starts well, few finish well, and only one stands on the highest podium to receive the gold medal. Don't be content with a T-shirt and a participant's pin when you could win the prize. The only applause that really matters is heard at the finish line. That is the applause to live and die for.

It is important to note here that in the spiritual realm we do not compete against one another in any way whatsoever! In fact, a sure way to lose that precious prize is to compete against your brothers and sisters. We fight the good fight against the world, the flesh (self), and the devil.

As in any race, keeping our attention on the goal line is of utmost importance. Focus is what keeps us going. Seeing the finish line stokes our motivation.

The writer of Hebrews said:

Therefore, since we have so great a cloud of witnesses surrounding us, let us also lay aside every encumbrance and the sin which so easily entangles us, and let us run with endurance the race that is set before us, fixing our eyes on Jesus, the author and perfecter of faith, who for the joy set before Him endured the cross, despising the shame, and has sat down at the right hand of the throne of God. For consider Him who has endured such hostility by sinners against Himself, so that you will not grow weary and lose heart. (Hebrews 12:1-3)

Our focus must be on Jesus, and Him alone. When we take our eyes off of Him and look to anything else, we will not have what it takes to cross that finish line well. We must consider what He endured for our sake to fire up the love in our souls necessary to endure for His sake and win this race.

Speaking about his lack of gifts or persuasiveness of personality, Paul said to the Corinthians, "For I determined to know nothing among you except Jesus Christ, and Him crucified" (1 Corinthians 2:2). This is the focus that keeps someone going for the whole race. Paul said to the Philippians, "To live is Christ and to die is gain" (Philippians 1:21).

All the other things we tend to focus on will not see us through. It may sound counterintuitive but even a personal desire to finish well is not enough by itself to actually accomplish the goal. Even the most noble of selfish desires will ultimately fail us. Jesus, and all He brings to us, is a treasure secure in heaven that no one can take from us. We don't have to earn this "gift of all gifts"—we never could. It has already been extended to us without strings.

It is only a love of Jesus that will see us through. That is something all of us can have, whether you are young or old, rich or poor, educated or not. All things, save for Jesus, will either fade over time or can be taken from us.

In the above text from Hebrews, we find some incredible encouragement. It says that Jesus is the author (starter) and finisher (completer) of our faith. We can imagine that Jesus was a good carpenter. Part of being a good craftsman is starting the job right, but what is especially important is to be good at finishing.

We know that when Jesus did anything, He did it better than people could imagine. The wine He made was the best wine. Paralytics rose and didn't walk with a limp but skipped and danced with full range of movement. Lepers' skin was as soft and smooth as a baby's after His touch. So, we know Jesus to be the best finisher, and it is His job, not yours, to finish your faith. He is the master carpenter, and we are His masterpiece (Ephesians 2:10). Think about that and give thanks. He can finish your faith to perfection.

Jesus starts and finishes our faith, so what is our part? It is not the quality or quantity of our faith that matters. Those are His concern. For us, it is the object of our faith that makes all the difference. When times are hard and people disappoint you, look at Jesus. When you have more bills yet to pay at the end of your paycheck, look at Jesus. When people reject you, look at Jesus. When you are tired and feel you cannot take another step on your journey, look at Jesus. He is the only one who can perfect your faith, and He wants that so much that He willingly died to do so. He has the desire, and He has the power—all we need do is direct our trust to Him. He will not force Himself on us; He is too good and kind to do that. He extends His hand with a generous offer, but we must be willing to accept it.

Jesus endured great hardships and made the ultimate sacrifice for us. His focus on the joy of being with us helped Him to not lose heart. Can we do the same?

Each of us has been given a calling, a destiny as unique to us as our own fingerprints. We not only received this special assignment, but we have also been given everything we need to accomplish it. We are lacking in nothing. We have been blessed with every spiritual blessing heaven can possibly offer (Ephesians 1:3). The wealth of heaven is already deposited into our account; now all we must do is believe it and mold our will to align with the calling God has given to us. Every step we take to fulfill that call will never be wasted, but we will always regret choosing to ignore that call.

All we require is the will, every day, to keep on pressing on. This is what we fight to do, so that one day we will hear our Lord say, "Well done, good and faithful slave. You were faithful with a few things, I will put you in charge of many things; enter into the joy of your master" (Matthew 25:21).

You Plus Jesus are Enough to Change the World

I've never been a great mathematician, but I have learned a couple of profound equations. The first is $0 + 0 = 0$. *Nothing* remarkable there—pardon the pun. This first equation becomes more revealing when it's followed by the second: $0 + \infty = \infty$. It is not the zero in the second equation that amounts to anything. It is the ∞—the infinite—that matters. Only when the infinite is added to the zero does the sum become significant—in fact, immeasurable. Left to ourselves, we all amount to zero. This was true even for Paul, and he says as much when he refers to the sum of all he brings to the equation as excrement (Philippians 3:7–8).

The author of Hebrews lists the great accomplishments of the people of faith from the Old Testament in chapter 11, then issues the charge we looked at above about focusing on Christ in our race. He then goes on to challenge us in chapter 13 to consider the lives of those who have walked before us and to imitate their faith. He says, "Remember those who led you, who spoke the word of God to you; and considering the result of their conduct, imitate their faith." This is the true heart of this book.

The very next words are: "Jesus Christ is the same yesterday, today, and *forever*." Another word for forever is "infinite." It is not that the people whose stories are told in the Old Testament are so exceptional. It is Jesus, the Infinite One, working through them who causes their lives to be remarkable and worthy of storytelling. Jesus hasn't changed. He is as much present with us here and now as He was then. All that is needed in this equation is a willing zero to become the next hero. That is what Paul was—a zero willing to join with the Infinite. Are you willing? Who knows what can happen in this world if you are willing to join without reservation to the Infinite One? If you think for a moment that you are not good enough for such a partnership, then you haven't been paying attention to the words in this chapter. If you are willing to surrender your future to Jesus, the outcome of your entire life will be beyond your imagination, regardless of the starting place. Be a willing zero, and you too can have a story that others will one day tell.

 **Final Journey Reflections**
We all will take this last journey, whether we are prepared or not. Why not be prepared? As we consider our final journey, here are some reflection questions to consider:

- What would finishing well look like to you?
- Who around you would you currently look to as a successor? What would it take for them to be ready?
- If you were to die today, what of your influence would carry on to the next generation?
- What do you need to start doing now so that your influence will go further and faster after your death?
- Are you living life in such a way that your story is worth telling?

We have seen that there is a tremendous price to pay if we want to finish well. That is probably the reason why so few do. Fulfilling our destiny is no accident. And finishing well is not just something that happens at the end of life. It happens every day. Like Paul, we must be willing to pay the price in the present for greater impact in the future. We must choose today to bend our will to that goal, and we must make the same choice every day. In a real sense, we must live as if every day were our last. Like Paul, we must decide today that we will finish well or die trying.

ENDNOTES

Acknowledgments

1. Roland Allen, *Missionary Methods: St. Paul's or Ours* (London: World Dominion Press, 1953).

2. J. Robert Clinton, *The Making of a Leader: Recognizing the Lessons and Stages of Leadership Development* (Colorado Springs, Colo.: IVP, 1988).

Introduction

1. David Alan Black, *Paul Apostle of Weakness: Astheneia and its Cognates in the Pauline Literature, Revised Ed.* (Eugene OR: Pickwick Publications 2012), p. xv.

2. J. Robert Clinton, *The Making of a Leader: Recognizing the Lessons and Stages of Leadership Development* (Colorado Springs, Colo.: Navpress, 1988), p. 30.

Chapter 1

1. Later Paul said of himself, "I was advancing in Judaism beyond many of my contemporaries among my countrymen, being more extremely zealous for my ancestral traditions" (Galatians 1:14).

2. Steve Jobs in a commencement address to the Stanford University Class of 2005.

3. Winston Churchill in an address to the British House of Commons, 1948.

4. I am indebted to Neil T. Andersen for the ways of being set free from the bondage of bitterness via forgiveness prescribed in this chapter, and I have used his excellent tool, *Seven Steps to Freedom*, throughout my ministry. See Neil T. Andersen, *Victory Over the Darkness: Realizing the Power of your Identity in Christ* (Ventura CA, Regal Press, 1990) pp. 203-205

Chapter 2

1. To see Luke as being sarcastic about Peter and the other eleven disciples not going out on mission in obedience to Jesus' command in Acts 1:8 is certainly a minority view. Most see Luke as being respectful throughout Acts and communicating a common purpose between Paul and Peter; I too think this is true. But there is also another message to be found in the story. Luke is very precise in his language, and he commonly omits much information if it doesn't contribute to his message. If we compare the first half of Acts, which focuses on Peter, with the second half, which focuses on Paul, we see a strong parallel. We see Peter and Paul engaged in very similar or even the same acts—raising a paraplegic, pronouncing judgment on a Jewish magician, raising the dead, making a thrilling nighttime escape from persecution, receiving visions and messages from the Lord, and giving bold sermons in the face of persecutors. Peter's shadow heals; Paul's handkerchief heals. I believe that the message here is that Paul's apostolic authority is equal to Peter's. Therefore, if this message is one purpose of Acts, then there certainly is merit in reading Acts 8:1 as I do. Luke is setting up the story to show that what Peter failed to do at that time, Paul went on to accomplish. Of course, Luke does portray the Jerusalem church as steadily declining in health over the course of the story, and it does not end well for the church. Eventually, following in Paul's example, Peter and the other eleven move into the mission fields as they were commanded to do.

2. Saul's conversion has been pivotal in history—an enemy of the Way becomes its greatest proponent who is willing to die for its veracity and goes on to establish the church among the Gentiles. Throughout history, many have attempted to refute the resurrection of Christ and the subsequent conversion of Saul but have become proponents of the faith they once tried to disprove. Among them are the law professor Simon Greenleaf and the Oxford scholar and author C. S. Lewis. The latter paradoxically describes his youthful years as a time when he was a hostile atheist "angry with God for not existing" (see C. S. Lewis, *Surprised by Joy: The Shape of My Early Life* (New York: Harcourt, 1956), p. 115). Paul's testimony still stands as persuasive proof of the resurrection of Christ. As

Lord Lyttleton once remarked, "The conversion and apostleship of St. Paul alone, duly considered, was of itself a demonstration sufficient to prove Christianity to be a divine revelation" (see George, Lord Lyttleton, *Observations on the Conversion and Apostleship of St. Paul: In a Letter to Gilbert West*, Esq. (London, 1747)). Lyttleton's entire book is digitized and available for free:

http://books.google.com/books?id=M54CAAAAQAAJ&print-sec=frontcover&dq=G.+Lyttleton+The+conversion+and+apostle-ship+of+St.+Paul&hl=en&ei=whRnTIHQCZ3YtAOdmqjqC-g&sa=X&oi=book_result&ct=result&resnum=1&ved=0CCoQ6A-EwAA#v=onepage&q&f=false

3. That Paul saw the Lord is verified by the accounts of Ananias (Acts 9:17) and Barnabas (Acts 9:27). It is probable that Saul's companions heard a loud noise but could not discern the words, much as the crowd heard a loud but indiscernible sound when the Father spoke to Jesus (John 12:29). According to the New American Standard Bible, Saul's companions could "not understand the voice of the One who was speaking" (Acts 22:9). Whatever they heard, the light, the reaction of Saul, and his resulting blindness must have been enough to cause them to take this event seriously and help Saul find a safe place to make sense of it.

4. Ananias, a disciple living in Damascus, was a devout Jew (Acts 22:12). He received a vision from the Lord telling him to go to Saul, heal him, and present to him his new calling. Ananias was hesitant, having heard of Saul and his notorious reputation, and so the Lord told him the details of Saul's conversion and new calling. The Lord also confirmed that Saul would experience suffering himself: "Go, for he is a chosen instrument of Mine, to bear My name before the Gentiles and kings and the sons of Israel; for I will show him how much he must suffer for My name's sake" (Acts 9:15-16).

5. See John Pollock, *The Apostle: A Life of Paul* (Colorado Springs, Colo.: Victor Books, 1985), p. 53.

6. Michael T. Cooper, *Ephesiology: A Study of the Ephesian Movement*, (Littleton, CO: William Carey Publishing, 2020), p. 49.

7. Deuteronomy 25:2–3 states that the maximum permissible number of lashes is forty, probably because more would be lethal. The Jews, always aware of the lines drawn by the Mosaic Law, reduced the number of lashes to thirty-nine; the Mishnah (Makkoth 3:10) prescribes the punishment as thirty-nine lashes to keep the punishers from overstepping the legal limit (if only through some accident of counting). Thirty-eight lashes would have been thought too few.

8. See Ralph Martin, *Word Biblical Commentary: 2 Corinthians* (Waco, Tex.: Word Books, 1986), pp. 376–77.

9. See Makkoth 3.2-11. The Talmud was not written down until much later than the New Testament, and so we cannot be entirely confident that the practices mentioned in the written Talmud were carried out during the 1st century exactly as prescribed there. Thus there are grounds for speculation, and of course some men may have acted unjustly in ways that suited their own agendas, as occurred a few times in the New Testament. Nevertheless, this is a good explanation for how Paul came to have so many floggings.

10. Pollock, *The Apostle*, p. 54 describes the scourging Paul would have endured five times over because of his deep love for his own people.

11. It is generally agreed that 2 Corinthians 11:25 (AD 56), where Paul mentions three shipwrecks, was written before Paul's shipwreck on his way to Rome, mentioned in Acts; therefore, Paul experienced at least four shipwrecks that we know of. Aren't you glad Paul wasn't around when we have air travel?

12. By this time, Stephen had been killed and Philip had settled in Caesarea so "the Seven" as they had been called probably were not as prominent in Jerusalem after the persecution that Saul led.

13. Many place this visit, mentioned in Galatians 2:1 ff., during the trip described in Acts 15, and this is also a viable explanation, though I personally prefer it here during this earlier trip because I think Galatians was penned before the council mentioned in Acts 15.

14. We could argue that this band was missing a feminine perspective. Leadership in later churches would have this important point of view as well (Acts 16:14–15, 17:4; Romans 16:1–16). Change comes in incremental steps, and each should be celebrated.

15. To learn more about the important equipping gifts given by Jesus to His church (Ephesians 4:11), read my book *Primal Fire: Reigniting the Church with the Five Gifts of Jesus* (Carol Stream: Tyndale Publishing House) 2014.

16. See Neil Cole, *Church 3.0: Upgrades for the Future of the Church* (San Francisco: Jossey-Bass, 2010), pp. 143-145, where I expound on the reasons why a leadership team of five is ideal.

17. J. Robert Clinton, *The Making of a Leader: Recognizing the Lessons and Stages of Leadership Development* (Colorado Springs, Colo.: IVP, 1988), p. 238.

Chapter 3
1. John Pollock, *The Apostle: A Life of Paul* (Colorado Springs, Colo.: Victor Books, 1985), p. 71.

2. Eckhard Schnabel, *Paul the Missionary: Realities, Strategies and Methods* (Downers Grove, Ill.: IVP, 2008), p. 79.

3. As an example of Luke's usage of *oikos* in the book of Acts, Cornelius is told to bring his household (*oikos*) together to hear a message from Peter (Acts 11:13–14). When Peter arrives, Cornelius is expecting him and has gathered his relatives and close friends (Acts 10:24), a group made up of more than just his immediate family and including the people

socially connected to him. We are told that the message was heard by a large gathering of people (Acts 11:13–14). Luke consistently demonstrates that the *oikos* was a primary means of spreading the message—with Lydia (Acts 16:15), the Philippian jailer (Acts 16:31), and Crispus (Acts 18:18). Luke also uses that word in Jesus' sermon about how to spread the good news of the Kingdom in his Gospel (Luke 10:5-7). Good news flies best on the wings of relationship.

4. See also Neil Cole, *Organic Church: Growing Faith Where Life Happens* (San Francisco: Jossey-Bass, 2005), pp. 162-169.

5. Eckhard Schnabel, *Early Christian Mission*, Vol. 2 (Downers Grove, Ill.: IVP, 2004), pp. 1084–88.

6. In Acts, Luke commonly summarizes what took place and then provides the details after the summary. We will delve further into Luke's style of writing in the next chapter where understanding it helps us makes sense of his narrative.

7. There is much debate about the chronology of Paul's three visits to Jerusalem and about his accounts mentioned in the Galatian epistle. I favor the view that if Paul had written the letter after his visit to Jerusalem, he would have mentioned the letter drafted by James regarding the subject, thus settling things once and for all. This is especially true given the portions of Galatians that specifically address his visits to Jerusalem and his interactions with the church's leadership but fails to mention these important events. It seems unrealistic that he would leave that information out of this letter given the letter's subject matter and overall purpose if it were written later. There are strong views on both sides of the issue, of course. I have chosen this chronology and share it here not in definitive language but in the language of probability.

Chapter 4

1. Many place the writing of letter to the Galatians later than this. I think that if the Jerusalem council had met before the letter was written,

the council's decision would have carried some weight in the letter. The meeting of that council goes unmentioned in Galatians, even though Paul mentions meetings with the leadership of the Jerusalem church with discussion specifically about the issue of Gentiles and Jews. To me a later letter is hard to reconcile.

2. It is indeed worth noting that Paul mentions his disappointment in Barnabas in this first letter he wrote to the Galatians prior to their splitting up (Galatians 2:13). This shows us that it was on his mind during this time where they were debating the next journey. He didn't shy away from shaming his partner to the very people they had just reached with the gospel and were intending to see face-to-face within a short time.

3. The original missionary band included John Mark but only while the missionaries were on Cyprus. Most of the work in the Galatian region was done by Paul and Barnabas alone, and so this new team was double in size. Luke did not mention his own name. He simply used the first-person plural in recounting those portions of the narrative in which he was a member of the group. This change in pronouns occurs twice in Acts and was Luke's humble way of revealing his involvement.

4. Luke's presence can be discerned by his use of the first-person plural (see note 3 above).

5. Paul, writing to the Philippian church later, would appeal to the members' sense of pride in their citizenship by reminding them that their citizenship was now in heaven (Philippians 3:20–21).

6. William M. Ramsay, *St. Paul: The Traveler and Roman Citizen*, rev. ed. (Grand Rapids, Mich.: Kregel, 2001), p. 174.

7. Granted, this is a puzzle, and I am trying to put the pieces together in a manner that makes sense. My conclusions are not definitive, but I believe that this is as good an explanation for these events as any and fits the pieces together best.

8. It is significant that Paul received a specific vision of the man. The man was clearly Macedonian, and Paul could see his entire body ("he was standing"). Maybe his accent revealed him to be Macedonian, but Luke's description seems to indicate that he recognized him as Macedonian from his appearance. Perhaps Paul was literally able to read the inscriptions on the jailer's uniform. One possible scenario is that Paul, upon seeing this man at the site of the beating, knew that he had to hold his tongue and endure the beating to gain access to this Macedonian man and help him and his household.

9. Although Luke's summation seems to indicate that Timothy stayed with Silas in Berea, other New Testament documents clarify that Timothy was in fact left in Thessalonica (1 Thessalonians 3:1–6). It is possible that Paul sent Timothy back to Thessalonica from Berea, since he himself went to Athens, leaving Silas in Berea. This possibility does not in any way change my proposition about Paul's shift in strategy from the first journey.

10. There is no doubt that Paul was constantly sending his team to strengthen the disciples and churches left in his wake (Philippians 2:19; 2 Timothy 4:12), and he specifically reminded the Thessalonians that he assigned Timothy to strengthen them in their new faith while he was at Athens by himself (1 Thessalonians 3:1-2). Later Paul would request Silas and Timothy to come join him, and they eventually did that after he started a work in Corinth without them.

11. William Barclay, *The New Daily Study Bible: The Acts of the Apostles* (Louisville, KY: Westminster John Knox Press, 2003), p. 152.

12. Johannes P. Louw and Eugene A. Nida, *Greek-English Lexicon of the New Testament Based on Semantic Domains*, Vol. 1, (NY, NY: United Bible Societies, 1988), p. 763.

13. Geoffrey W. Bromiley et al. (eds.), *The International Standard Bible Encyclopedia*, Vol. 1 (Grand Rapids, Mich.: Eerdmans, 1978), pp. 287–88.

14. At this point, navigating Acts is a challenge. Luke interrupted the chronological flow with parenthetical summations and then got back into the chronological flow to relay some of the details. He did something similar for the first journey when he summarized how Paul and Barnabas went from town to town preaching (Acts 14:6–7) and then jumped back into describing the details of what happened (Acts 14:8 ff.). As a result, I find it illogical to follow the chapter verse by verse in strictly chronological fashion, although it is progressive. I believe that Luke described Paul's Corinthian experience by first giving a general summation and telling how the events there took place and how the work started (Acts 18:1–8). Then, in a parenthetical thought, he got specific about two things—what occurred to get the work started and how long it would last (Acts 18:9–11). The narration then went into more detail about how the work concluded (Acts 18:12–18). It would make no sense for Jesus to tell Paul to "not be silent" in the middle of very fruitful advances well into a rapidly expanding movement. The next statement—"And he settled there a year and six months"—indicates an overall parenthetical summation tied specifically to the previous thought regarding Paul's nighttime vision of Jesus. In other words, Paul saw Jesus, and as a result he stayed in Corinth for a year and six months, which is how all of this happened. Luke then dove back into specifics to show us what gets us to the end. Another parenthetical paragraph slipped in at the end of this chapter (Acts 18:24–28) is equally hard to place precisely in its chronology, but I hope in this book to clarify the placement of that paragraph.

15. The Isthmian Games, much like the Olympiad, were held for centuries in the years before and after the Olympic Games and always took place in Corinth. A winner received a wreath of celery or woven pine needles, which Paul alludes to in his letter to the Corinthians (1 Corinthians 9:25).

16. Many commentators assume that Priscilla and Aquila were already believers, but that is not necessarily true. This is still early for there to be Christians in Rome. Luke states that they were Jews, not followers of the

Way. There is no mention of them being baptized, but we have already seen (Acts 17:33–34) that Luke does not always mention the baptism of new converts when they believed. I think that Luke is describing Paul living out the new insights he has received from Jesus, and that these are the first of many people He will have in this city. Luke tells us that Aquila and Priscilla have come to Corinth because they were exiled from Rome by the emperor's edict banishing Jews. Many believe that they were exiled from Rome because of their faith in Christ, after Claudius's imperial edict in AD 49–50. The edict, commonly referred to as the one identified by Suetonius in his *Life of Claudius* (24.4), refers to "Jews [who] were indulging in constant riots at the instigation of Chrestus, [whom] he banished from Rome" *Chrestus* is often assumed to be a reference to Christ but there is no hard evidence. The thought is that the Romans might have believed that Jesus was a Jewish rebel stirring up riots between the traditional Jews and the new sect. There is certainly some merit to this proposition, which makes it likely that Aquila and Priscilla became Christians before meeting Paul, but Luke does not state as much. Luke tells us plainly that they were banished from Rome because they were "Jews" (Acts 18:2). Given Luke's obvious bias, it does seem unlikely that he would say they were exiled because they were "Jews" if indeed it was for their faith in Christ. The description found in the edict certainly does not reflect either our Lord or His followers, but when did the edicts of secular governments ever reflect the righteousness of God or His people? Whether Aquila and Priscilla became Christ-followers before or after they met Paul, he certainly influenced them, and a lifelong partnership in spreading the gospel was begun.

17. Luke simply says, "And having spent some time there, he left."

18. Luke does mention that Apollos was learned in the Scriptures and "was instructed in the way of the Lord" but only familiar with John's baptism. This could mean that he was not familiar with the practice of believer's or disciple's baptism, but only a baptism of repentance. One can argue from the book of Acts that baptism is tied directly to an understanding of the gospel and salvation. Aquila and Priscilla certainly

recognized Apollos's profound giftedness and passion but also his incorrect understanding. They explained more of who Christ is and what He had done. It is plausible that Apollos knew about Christ before meeting these two and simply misunderstood a nonessential doctrine, for there was a church in his hometown of Alexandria. But Luke makes it clear that Apollos had limited knowledge of Christ and that he was influenced by the teaching of John the Baptist. For Luke to make mention of the correction suggests that it was more than just a few blanks with respect to nonessential doctrines. Perhaps Apollos was acquainted with Jesus as Messiah and even as a substitutionary atonement, as John was (John 1:29), but did not yet know of His death, burial, or resurrection. If so, then his message would have been that of repentance and righteousness—perhaps even of following Christ—but without the gospel, his ministry would have lacked power for salvation (Romans 1:16). This would certainly best fit the description presented by Luke. It is not by coincidence that Luke goes on, in the very next paragraph, to describe in some detail other disciples of John the Baptist, showing that they had not understood the gospel or received the Holy Spirit. It is not unreasonable that Apollos was in the same place. Regardless, Apollos was deficient in his understanding of the work of Christ and was quite responsive to the tutelage of Aquila and Priscilla, who were mentored by Paul. The results still come out to be an astonishing reproduction of Paul's ministry practice, passed on through three generations. It is of note to see the influence of John the Baptist spreading around the globe.

19. Luke had a habit of filling his parchment. His Gospel and Acts are the longest books of the New Testament in terms of length (not the number of chapters but the number of words), and together they amount to about half of the New Testament. Some scholars believe that for both volumes, Luke wrote until he reached the end of the parchment.

20. Brad has since planted many churches and founded Kingdom Causes, which is expanding into multiple cities and municipalities bringing Kingdom transformation where it is so badly needed today. http://kingdomcauses.org

21. I recommend two classics by the British author C. S. Lewis: *The Problem of Pain* (San Francisco: HarperSanFrancisco, 2001) and *A Grief Observed* (San Francisco: HarperSanFrancisco, 2001). See also Philip Yancey, *Where Is God When It Hurts?* (Grand Rapids, Mich.: Zondervan, 1977).

Chapter 5

1. J. Robert Clinton, *The Making of a Leader: Recognizing the Lessons and Stages of Leadership Development* (Colorado Springs, Colo.: IVP, 1988), p. 46.

2. "Tyrannus" can also be translated as tyrant (someone who rules unjustly or oppressively). Ephesus had its own philosopher many centuries prior to Paul named Heraclitus, who was said to be quite a demanding and negative personality. It is possible that this school of philosophy took on the identity and name of his demeanor. That is another theory about this school, though I favor the theory mentioned in the pages above.

3. Michael T. Cooper, *Ephesiology: A Study of the Ephesian Movement*, (Littleton, CO: William Carey Publishing, 2020), pp. 86, 47-48.

4. Kirsopp Lake and Henry Joel Cadbury (eds.), *The Beginnings of Christianity*, part 1: *The Acts of the Apostles*, vol. 4: *English Translation and Commentary* (London: Macmillan, 1933), p. 239.

5. These two-plus years, combined with the three months spent working out of the synagogue, came to about three years in total (Acts 20:31); see F. F. Bruce, *The Book of the Acts*, rev. ed. (Grand Rapids, Mich.: Eerdmans, 1988), p. 366.

6. William Barclay, *The New Daily Study Bible: The Acts of the Apostles* (Louisville: John Knox Press, 1975), pp. 164–65.

7. Just before World War II, Adolf Hitler relocated this altar to Berlin, where it remains to this day in the Pergamum Museum. The altar was

considered by some to be the "throne of Satan," and Hitler was in search of occult artifacts that he thought could grant him power.

8. In modern museums there are many samples of these sorts of magical papyri. Bruce, *The Book of the Acts*, p. 369, cites London, Paris, and Leiden as the places where the largest collections of such papyri are found. Princeton University also has a sample, translated by and expounded upon by the Greek scholar B. M. Metzger, "St. Paul and the Magicians," *Princeton Seminary Bulletin* 38 (1944), pp. 27–30.

9. It is interesting that the word used to describe this riotous mob is *ekklesia*, which is the word our Bible translates as "church." This group of highly energized, angry people shouting their praise and worship to a false god may be the largest "church" gathering mentioned in the New Testament. I think I've been to that church before. Could this be the only model of a large church worship service found in our Bibles? Something to think about.

10. In the first chapter of *One Thing*, I compare the "good" church (the Galatians) to the "bad" church (the Corinthians). I show that while Corinth had severe moral and social issues, Paul wrote to them with much more compassion and kindness. One of Paul's favorite terms used to describe the people he wrote to was *hagioi*, "saints" or "holy ones." He said it of the Corinthians eleven times. Even though his letters to them are said to be "strong" and "causing sorrow," they are not nearly as strong as the letter he wrote to the "good" church trying to obey the Law—the Galatians. Paul never had a kind word to say to the Galatians but called them "foolish Galatians," "bewitched," and "separate from Christ." He says of them that all their works are "cursed." The Galatian letter is the only one where Paul does not use the term "saints." See Cole, Neil, *One Thing: A Revolution to Change the World with Love* (Nashville, TN: Thomas Nelson), 2016, pp. 3-21. One can hope, after four personal visits and two letters (one from Paul and one from the Jerusalem church), the Galatian disciples improved.

11. Today we have the second and third letters that Paul wrote, now labeled the first and the second respectively, but the first one is lost (1 Corinthians 5:9).

Chapter 6

1. Many consider this a reference to his standing before Caesar during his second and last Roman imprisonment, when he wrote the epistle to Timothy. I personally believe that this is a reference to his first trial before Caesar, which occurred during his fourth journey, because he was delivered during that defense, not during his last one.

2. I have intentionally written these questions from our point of view and in the language of our own context. I am certain that the Jews in Paul's day would have couched these issues in entirely different language.

3. In Acts 10:27–29, Peter tells Cornelius that it is unlawful for him as a Jew to enter a Gentile home. But this was from oral law, not the Mosaic Law, which indicates some confusion. This is what also led him in Antioch to separate from the Gentiles at meals (Galatians 2:11–21)

4. Of course, when we read Galatians (written after Paul's first journey) and Romans (written shortly before this visit to Jerusalem), it is easy for us to see how this rumor may have gained momentum. Paul's view of the Law and the Jerusalem church's view of the Law were probably very different by this time.

5. Flavius Josephus, *Antiquities of the Jews* 20:198.

6. From a portion of the letter from Ignatius to the Ephesian church. https://www.newadvent.org/fathers/0104.htm

Chapter 7

1. Eckhard Schnabel, *Paul the Missionary: Realities, Strategies and Methods* (Downers Grove, Ill.: IVP, 2008), p. 116.

2. The information about miles traveled by Paul is from Schnabel, *Paul the Missionary: Realities, Strategies and Methods* (Downers Grove, Ill.: IVP, 2008), p. 122. For the shipwrecks, see note 11 to Chapter 2. With respect to churches that Paul started in his lifetime, some have said that there were only fourteen, but I would assume that several other churches were also started but not necessarily named as churches. For instance, there is no mention of a church started in Athens, but there were households there that began to follow Christ, and so we can assume that a church was born there. In Philippi, there were two households that accepted the gospel, and so there could have been two house churches there. Some say that there was just one church in Philippi, because Paul wrote a letter to its members, but the letter is "to the saints in Christ who are in Philippi." We have already noted that he started only the Ephesian church in Asia Minor, which in turn started many others. But in both Ephesus and in Corinth there were many house churches who were the recipients of his letters. There are also places where no churches are mentioned, but we do know that Paul was preaching and households were responsive in those places (for example, in Illyricum, Cyprus, Crete, Malta, Damascus, Arabia, and perhaps even Spain). Did he start churches while he was in Tarsus? Acts does mention churches in Syria (Acts 15:40–41). He probably started close to twenty churches himself, with many more born from those. Finally, regarding the two letters written by Paul that are not in the New Testament, his actual first letter to the Corinthians is mentioned in the letter that we now call 1 Corinthians (1 Corinthians 5:9), and his letter to the Laodiceans is also mentioned in the letter to the Colossians (Colossians 4:16).

3. Daniel, Nehemiah, and some of the historical books of the Old Testament were written in palaces. Most of the minor prophets, many of David's psalms and Paul's letters, as well as John's book of Revelation were written when the authors were on the run or in prison. David wrote from both palaces and places of hiding.

4. J. Robert Clinton, *The Making of a Leader Second Edition: Recognizing the Lessons and Stages of Leadership Development*, (Carol Stream, IL, Navpress, 2012) p. 242.

ABOUT THE AUTHOR

Neil Cole was born and raised in Los Angeles, California. While studying art at California State University, Long Beach, he encountered the good news of Jesus Christ and turned his life over to Him, never looking back.

Neil's journey in God's Kingdom brought him to serve in a megachurch of over 3,500 people, in a local community church of 100, and now as a catalyst to help start tens of thousands of small, rapidly multiplying, organic churches that meet in homes, campuses, prisons, dormitories, and places of business across the globe. Neil has authored eighteen books (translated into fifteen languages) and traveled to over fifty nations, sowing the seeds of God's Kingdom, catalyzing the development of organic church movements, and coaching thousands of leaders and churches.

Neil has been married for over forty years to Dana, and they have three adult children—Heather, Erin, and Zach—and six grandkids.

www.ingramcontent.com/pod-product-compliance
Lightning Source LLC
Chambersburg PA
CBHW060514130626
46553CB00002B/496